The Day That Cries Forever

The Day That Cries Forever

Stories of the Destruction of Chenega
During the 1964 Alaska Earthquake

∿∿

Collected and Edited by
John E. Smelcer

Foreword by
Charles W. Totemoff

Chenega Future, Inc.
Anchorage, Alaska

Copyright 2006 by Chenega Future, Inc.

Pre-1964 photographs copyright by John Poling Trust

All rights reserved. No part of this book may be reproduced in any form without the expressed permission of the publisher, with the exception of educational use.

Direct all questions to: Shareholder Relations, Chenega Corporation, 3000 C Street, Suite 301, Anchorage, Alaska 99503-3975

10-digit ISBN 1-57833-325-3
13-digit ISBN 9871578333257

This project was supported by a grant from the Alaska Humanities Forum, part of the National Endowment for the Humanities.

Text design by RedLine Books

Manufactured in the United States of America

Order additional copies from Todd Communications, 203 W. 15th Ave., Suite 102, Anchorage, AK 99501

Order online at www.alaskabooksandcalendars.com

CONTENTS

Foreword by Charles W. Totemoff, vii
Introduction by John E. Smelcer, viii

Margaret Borodkin	*Voices in the Darkness,* 1
Steve Eleshansky	*The End of Days,* 4
Larry Evanoff	*On Hearing the News,* 7
Bill Hjort	*Russian Orthodox Celebrations,* 9
Karen Selanoff Katelnikoff	*Memories Left Behind,* 13
Avis Kompkoff	*Premonitions of Things Yet to Come,* 17
Carol Ann Kompkoff	*The Longest Night,* 20
Donald P. Kompkoff, Sr.	*The Long Road Ahead,* 22
Mary Ann Kompkoff	*The Calm before the Storm,* 24
Nick Kompkoff, Jr.	*A Force of Nature,* 27
Paul Kompkoff, Jr.	*The Short-Lived Days of Summer,* 30
Pete Kompkoff, Jr.	*Chenega Days,* 32
Henry Makarka	*The Long Summer of Clams,* 38
Andy Selanoff	*Villagers without a Village,* 41
Kenny Selanoff	*And the Waters Shall Come,* 49
Paul Timothy Selanoff	*The Day I Was Alone, but Not Alone,* 54
Jessie Tiedeman	*A Twist of Fate,* 60
Maggie A. Totemoff	*What Will Remain,* 62
Michael John Vigil	*The Unforgotten,* 64
Donia M. Abbott	*Touched My Generation,* 67

Notes on the Contributors, 73

ILLUSTRATIONS

Photo I-1, *Mercalli Intensity Scale map*, xii
Photo I-2, *Government Hill Elementary School*, xiii
Photo 1, *Tatitlek, Alaska*, 6
Photo 2, *Russian Orthodox Church*, 9
Photo 3, *Chenega Village (west)*, 10
Photo 4, *Chenega Village (east)*, 11
Photo 5, *Chenega Village schoolhouse*, 14
Photo 6, *A school class portrait*, 15
Photo 7, *Aerial view of Chenega Village, 1964*, 19
Photo 8, *Cooperative store*, 30
Photo 9, *The dock, viewed from the store*, 31
Photos 10 & 11, *Chenega across the seasons*, 33
Photo 12, *Iceberg at the store dock*, 34
Photo 13, *A Nellie Juan boat*, 36
Photo 14, *Bidarka construction shop*, 41
Photo 15, *A fully loaded, sea-going bidarka*, 42
Photo 16, *Fish from the sea*, 65
Photo 17, *Chenega Village schoolhouse, 1997*, 68

Foreword

For the past several years there has been a growing concern among shareholders about the loss of our language, customs, and subsistence traditions. In the spring and summer of 2004, interested shareholders began a grassroots effort to do something about the slow erosion of our culture. Twice they assembled in Anchorage to discuss the problems and to define long-term goals and objectives. From those meetings, the Sugcestun Language and Cultural Preservation Project was established. One of the first priorities was to document first-person accounts by survivors of the tsunamis that devastated the old village of Chenega during the 1964 Good Friday Alaska Earthquake. That singular event was a turning point in Chenega's history. Twenty-five years later to the day, Chenega was again devastated by disaster when the *Exxon Valdez* wrecked on Bligh Reef, spilling eleven million gallons of crude oil into Prince William Sound, negatively impacting our subsistence way of life for many years afterward.

This book is the product of our determination and commitment to preserve our heritage. The Board of Directors of Chenega Corporation has been honored to support this project, providing financial assistance to conduct the first two Anchorage workshops. It should be noted that royalties from this book will go toward scholarships for Chenega shareholders and their descendants.

Charles W. Totemoff,
President and CEO, Chenega Corporation

Introduction

On Good Friday, March 27, 1964, the largest earthquake ever to strike North America shook the state of Alaska for a full four minutes. The destructive power was tremendous. Coastal communities in south-central Alaska were hardest hit; and while much has been written about Anchorage, Valdez, and Seward, very little has been written about the tiny Native Village of Chenega, which was completely obliterated by a series of massive tsunamis generated by the earthquake.

More than a quarter of the population perished in the waves.

Before the earthquake, Chenega was a small, island community of about 120 people speaking the now-endangered Sugcestun Sugpiaq regional dialect of the broader Alutiiq language that is more akin to Yupik than to its geographically neighboring language, Aleut. Like all Alaska native languages, it had no written form until recently. For Sugcestun, most language documentation began in the early 1970s. The name of the village, *Chenega,* means *along the side* (from the word *caniqaq),* referring to its geographic location on the side of the island. People from neighboring villages often called Chenega *Ing'im Atca* (from the word *ing'iq),* a nickname meaning *under the mountain,* referring to the village's location below a mountain.

The original village was the oldest continuously inhabited native community in the area of Prince William Sound. The name of the village was first reported by Ivan Petroff and appears in the 1880 Russian-Alaska census. It is known that Vitus Bering, the famous Russian discoverer of Alaska, spent time moored off the shores of Chenega. Later, Lord Baranov, then governor of Russian-America, married Anna of Chenega, making her the first "First Lady of Alaska."

Introduction

For the most part, the people of Chenega lived a subsistence lifestyle, fishing the sea, hunting seals, and gathering shellfish, bird eggs, and berries. As well, they became known as a people of deep spiritual conviction after Russian fur traders brought the Russian Orthodox Church to Alaska. Even today, a beautiful, new church stands as the pride of the community's rebuilt village in Chenega Bay.

While Anchorage, Seward, and Valdez rebuilt after the earthquake, the survivors of Chenega never returned to live at their ancestral home because of government-imposed relocation. Some survivors do not openly or willingly discuss that tragic day. To them, it is an unspeakable matter, better kept inside. To others, the pain of having lost loved ones, even forty years ago, is still too great. Because of these feelings, this project has met with resistance. Some survivors have refused to participate, and their feelings are understandable and must be respected.

Another reason why the old village of Chenega was relocated was simply due to geography. Clearly, the old village was situated in a bad location, in the event of another tsunami. The new village of Chenega Bay is built on Evan's Island and situated on a much higher elevation above sea level. After decades of struggling to determine a new village site, the citizens of Chenega have a new hope of rebuilding a strong community rooted in tradition and family.

One of the unforeseen effects of dislocation is that the people are losing their indigenous language. In a close-knit and somewhat isolated community, language—even an endangered language—can survive, precariously. But when indigenous people of Chenega moved away to different villages and towns and cities, the community of language was also, in great measure, affected. Today, very few people speak the old tongue. Fortunately, there is a movement afoot to revitalize the language.

The stories in this volume reflect the memories of many people. Some were adults at the time, while others were yet children. Some were not in Chenega during the event itself, though their homes were lost. Two younger people, for instance, were away at a boarding school in Wrangell, and one was not even born at the time; yet all of their lives were similarly affected.

The stories were collected over a year's time in a variety of ways using a variety of media. Some were audio-taped in personal interviews with the editor; family members recorded others in the comfortable familiarity of their own homes, sending them to the editor for transcription; several were written out by hand; and two were e-mailed. The editor has been careful to maintain the original contents of the stories, as well as the oral emphases and inflections of the storytellers (to the extent possible in written language), even when that meant transgressing precise rules of written English grammar and punctuation. Nevertheless, clarifications were frequently needed, and indeed, requested. In fact, every story went through a multistage approval process. Each storyteller reviewed the first transcription of his or her narrative. Then subsequent drafts, including the final draft, were again approved at meetings held in Anchorage throughout the year.

There is no linear progression to the telling of this sorrowful episode in the history of a people. No single story is more important than any other. Events happened to everyone at the same time. Thus, each personal account is but a snapshot of the whole picture. Because of this, the narratives have been arranged alphabetically by last name, except for Donia Abbott's story, which has been placed at the end because she was not yet born at the time of the quake. No attempt has been made to arrange recorded events for rhetorical purposes. These personal stories speak eloquently for themselves.

While many books and articles have been written about the 1964 Good Friday Alaska Earthquake, even recently, the tragic story of Chenega has been mostly forgotten. Without it, as former Alaskan Governor Jay Hammond insists, the story of Alaska's history is incomplete.

1964 Alaska Earthquake

The 1964 Good Friday Alaska Earthquake occurred on March 27, 1964. Originally recorded at a magnitude of 8.5 on the Richter scale, geologists later reexamined the evidence and increased the Good Friday magnitude to 9.2 Mw (moment magnitude), making it the second most powerful earthquake in history. The 1960 earthquake in Chile

Introduction

was slightly higher at 9.5 on the Richter scale, and an earthquake of unknown magnitude that jolted Tokyo in 1923 may have been more powerful. Almost a million people were killed or injured in that quake and subsequent tsunamis. More than 1,200 aftershocks followed during the next month.

The epicenter of the Alaska Earthquake was at 61.04 degrees north latitude by 147.73 degrees west longitude, approximately eighty miles east of Anchorage (fifty-five miles west of Valdez), near College Fjord at the edge of the Gulf of Alaska on the Fairweather Fault, which is part of the boundary between the Pacific and North American tectonic plates. The rupture occurred at a depth of fourteen to fifteen miles into the earth's crust. The cause of the 1964 Alaska earthquake was the northwest movement of the Pacific Plate, which generally moves at a rate of two to three inches each year (5-7 cm.), causing the crust of southern Alaska to become compressed and warped. From this activity, some areas along the coast become compressed while others are uplifted. Every so many hundreds of years—or even thousands—the sudden southeastward movement of parts of Alaska's coast violently relieves this compression. Such was the case in the 1964 event, and it is bound to happen again. Such is the unpredictable nature of the highly volatile tectonic Pacific zone, the northern-most arc of the "Ring of Fire," a region of volcanic and earthquake activity that encircles the entire Pacific Ocean, including New Zealand, South America, and Japan. According to the University of Alaska, Fairbanks, Seismology Department, Alaska experiences 24,000 earthquakes each year, accounting for more than a tenth of the world's total.

Besides the Richter scale, another means of measuring earthquakes is called the Mercalli Intensity Scale, a rating system that calculates major structural damage and ground fissures and failures. This is a twelve-point scale ranging from I to XII: I indicating that the seismic event was not felt, XII indicating total destruction with the loss of many lives. The 1964 Alaska Earthquake measured XI at its maximum intensity nearest the epicenter and VIII–X in Anchorage, Seward, and Valdez. By the time the effects reached Fairbanks, it was downgraded to VI, and it rated III–IV by the time it hit the Arctic coast. (This classification

The Day That Cries Forever

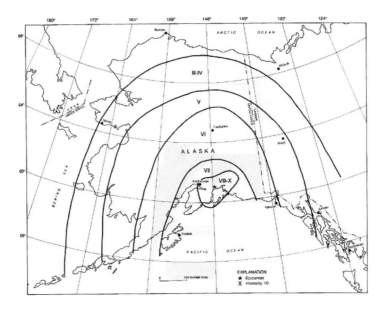

I-1. Mercalli Intensity Scale map, showing VIII–X intensity levels of the 1964 quake in the Ancorage area, lessening intensities beyond

means that most of the people who felt the quake were distributed over an enormous area of the Pacific Northwest, far from the epicenter, and experienced relatively little damage.) Similar rating systems exist for other natural disasters. For example, the Fujita Scale measures the intensity and destructive potential of tornadoes on a scale of F0–F5.

As a result of the earthquake, almost a mile (four thousand feet) of waterfront property in Valdez, including 97 million cubic yards of soil material, collapsed into the sea, and half a mile of Seward's coastline slid into the bay amid burning oil slicks caused by damaged fuel storage tanks. The Latouche Islands displaced about fifty feet to the southeast; portions of Montague Island were uplifted twelve to twenty-seven feet; and the area around Portage down-dropped as much as nine feet. (You can see the effect along the Seward Highway as you near the Portage Glacier turnoff). On the whole, the Pacific Plate subducted beneath the North American Plate some twenty-seven feet on average.

Introduction

During the four minutes of the earthquake, the violent shaking was so intense and widespread that significant damage covered about 130,000 square kilometers in Alaska, and people felt the earth trembling over an area of about 1.3 million square kilometers. The event triggered avalanches and landslides. An entire segment of the Million Dollar Bridge, which crosses the lower Copper River above Cordova, collapsed. (Restoration began in the summer of 2003.) Indeed, the effects of the earthquake reached as far south as Oregon and northern California. But no place was as hard hit as south-central Alaska in port towns such as Anchorage, Valdez, and Seward. Witnesses said they thought it was the end of the world.

The aftershock zone that followed the main earthquake was about 250–300 kilometers wide and extended about 800 kilometers from Prince William Sound to Kodiak Island. On the first day following the main quake, there were eleven aftershocks with a magnitude greater than 6.0 on the Richter scale. Thousands of smaller aftershocks were recorded in the month that followed, and even smaller aftershocks continued over the next year.

I-2. Government Hill Elementary School in Anchorage, following the 1964 earthquake

As large as the earthquake was, only 131 people lost their lives—115 in Alaska and 16 in Oregon and California. (Numbers vary slightly in different sources.) For an earthquake of its size, this was a very small death toll, largely because so few people lived in that portion of Alaska in 1964 and because the earthquake happened at 5:36 P.M. on a holiday, a time when most people were at home preparing for dinner. If it had struck on a weekday during regular workday hours—when children were at school, men and women at work, and street traffic heavy—the death toll would certainly have been substantially higher. Government Hill Elementary School, for instance, broke in two, one half falling some fifteen feet to its resting place in a heap. Whole sections of streets in Anchorage collapsed, dropping automobiles into holes ten to fifteen feet deep. Indeed, some thirty blocks of Anchorage were severely damaged or destroyed.

Landslides, caused by liquefaction of the soil, created much of the damage. The violent shaking for so long a duration caused soil and sand (mixing with groundwater) to behave as liquid. In effect, the ground turned into mud and gave way under the pressure of the earthquake and gravity. Subsequent landslides destroyed seventy-five homes in Turnagain Heights, then a popular residential area in Anchorage overlooking the waters of Cook Inlet. The ground liquefaction also disrupted various city services, including telephone, water, sewer, gas, and electricity.

Property damage in Alaska was estimated at $84.3 million in 1964 dollars. In today's economy the damage would likely be put at $400 to $500 million. Overall, taking into account the damage from the quake itself, after shocks, and tsunamis in the wide area affected, the damage would likely be assessed at $1.5 billion in modern dollars. If a 9.2 earthquake were to strike Los Angeles or San Francisco today, with their dense populations, tens of thousands of residents might perish in the aftermath, and the cost in property damage would certainly approach a hundred billion dollars.

The 1964 earthquake impacted much of Alaska, British Columbia, Washington, Oregon, and Northern California. Even Texas and Florida measured vertical motions of two to four inches, and long-period seis-

Introduction

mic waves traveled around the world for several weeks after the main event. Dr. Doug Christensen, a scientist at the University of Alaska Fairbanks Geophysical Institute, likens this series of seismic vibrations to that of a church bell ringing. Readings were measured as far away as northern Australia, New Zealand, and western Argentina.

Tsunami

Although the earthquake itself did significant damage, another devastating effect was the creation of a tsunami, a giant oceanic wave generated by tectonic uplifting of the sea floor. The Aleutian-Alaska megathrust zone, an enormous tectonic region encompassing almost the entire northern-most Pacific Oceanic land-sea boundary, is a region in which tsunamigenesis—the creation of tsunamis—can pose extreme danger along coastal areas. The uplifting of the sea floor displaces water volume, similar to when a person steps into a bathtub filled to the very brim with water. The suddenness of the uplifting movement imparts energy and velocity to the water as it is displaced. The ensuing open-ocean sea wave races toward land at high speeds and builds to terrific heights. Although the elevation diminishes as the wave comes up against the shallower waters of the continental shelf, the destructive force of the incoming water can be devastating.

As a result of the 1964 Alaska Earthquake, the open-ocean tsunami measured an astounding 210 feet tall in Valdez Arm. That's a wall of seawater about the height of a twenty-story building racing across the surface of the ocean. As the Good Friday Earthquake was the second largest in history, so too was the tsunami it generated the second largest ever recorded. Because there were a series of earthquakes, there was a subsequent series of tsunamis. Data and witness testimony indicate that there were four series of tsunami waves. The first of the four hit the mainland within twenty minutes of the initial earthquake.

As the speeding wave of a tsunami crashes into a landmass, it can actually climb uphill higher than its crest. This is called run-up. The heights of run-up measurements varied around the state: eighteen feet on Kodiak Island, twenty-seven feet at Valdez, seventy-five feet at Blackstone Bay, and well near one hundred feet tall at Chenega, then a small village of about 120 people—almost all Alaska natives—living in Prince William Sound, where they had lived for countless generations.

Fortunately, the earthquake happened during low tide, which contributed to a lower death toll statewide. If the tide had been high, the tsunami run-up would certainly have been higher and would have taken more lives and inflicted more property damage in towns like Valdez and Seward. The main tsunami wave was so large that it was measured as far away as Antarctica (though it took almost twenty hours to reach that far and measured less than a foot).

Another kind of earthquake effect is called a seiche and occurs when a tsunami wave enters an enclosed body of water such as a bay, harbor, or lake. The repeated sloshing back and forth is much like the effect from jumping into a swimming pool; the initial displacement wave races across the pool, strikes the opposing concrete pool wall (thereby losing a portion of its energy), and bounces back, getting smaller and smaller with each cycle. This effect was felt as far away as South Africa, where oscillations were observed in the height of water in wells.

Because of the enormous destructive power inherent in tsunamis and because future such cataclysmic events will have the potential for far greater destruction of life and property than experienced in the Good Friday Earthquake of 1964 (Anchorage's population has grown to over 250,000 people, and Valdez now stockpiles millions of barrels of oil pumped from Prudhoe Bay via the Alaska Pipeline), the federal government has established the West Coast & Alaska Tsunami Warning Center located in Palmer, a town about thirty miles northeast of Anchorage. Established in 1967, the center monitors seismic and tsunamigenic activity in the Pacific Ocean off the coast of Alaska. The highly computerized center exists to mitigate tsunami dangers by immediately issuing warnings to emergency preparedness agencies in the coastal states of the Pacific Northwest and British Columbia in hopes that timely warnings over a variety of public media will save lives in the future.

Introduction

Nowadays, families travel by boat to the old village of Chenega each Memorial Day to visit those they lost, be it son or daughter, brother or sister, mother or father, grandparent, uncle, aunt, or cousin. They go to remember, pray, cry, apologize, rejoice, heal, and accept. They hold Russian Orthodox services, tidy graves, distribute flowers, tell stories, picnic, and try to regain the sense of belonging—a reunification of community. Some are too young to remember the old village, and some are too old to forget.

But always—always—to the people of Chenega, March 27, 1964, will remain impressed upon their collective memory as a day that cries forever. These are their stories—stories that have been untold for too long, and their eventual telling has been slow, difficult, and painful.

This book is lovingly dedicated to the twenty-six people of Chenega who lost their lives in the 1964 Alaska Earthquake and Tsunami:

Anna Vlasoff	Dora Jackson
William Evanoff	Cindy Ribaloff
Sally Evanoff	Danny Ribaloff
Joanne Kompkoff	Arvella Jackson
Willie Kompkoff	Sally Eleshansky
Daria Kompkoff	Steve Eleshansky, Sr.
Richard Kompkoff	Rhonda Eleshansky
Phillip Totemoff, Jr.	Julia Ann Kompkoff
Billy Selanoff	Norma Jean Kompkoff
Jeanne Selanoff	Robert Selanoff
Jack Evanoff	Tommy Selanoff
Nellie Evanoff	Alex Chimovisky
Emmanuel Chimovisky	Anna Chimovisky

Vechnaya Pamyat   Memory Eternal

Margaret Borodkin
Voices in the Darkness

It was around suppertime when the earthquake hit. The tidal waves didn't come right away after that. It took a little while for them to travel to Chenega.

I was thirty-five in 1964. I remember I was at my mother's house. I think we had just finished eating. They were going to play a movie up at the schoolhouse. I don't remember what it was called, but some people still remember. I do know that if the earthquake had happened even an hour later, almost everyone in the village would have been up the hill watching that movie.

Maybe a lot fewer people would have died then.

When the first earthquake began, the whole house was shaking. The walls were splitting, and part of the roof and ceiling was falling in. Things on shelves or tables were crashing to the floor. I tried to get out of the house, but when I went under a doorway, something heavy fell on me and trapped me on the floor. My leg and hip hurt really badly. I thought my leg was broken. I couldn't get up. When the shaking stopped, I could see my mother outside. She was yelling to people to come help me. After a few minutes I began to hear a loud sound. It was really loud. I couldn't see because I was trapped on the floor, but it must have been the giant tidal wave. When it struck the house, it was as if a bomb blew up. Everything was crashing and rolling and smashing. I must have passed out during that because I don't remember anything else about that. I just remember being scared.

When I woke up I was out in the bay floating on a large piece of debris. I don't even remember what it was exactly–the wall of a house,

I think. There was lots of other debris floating on the surface around me. The whole bay was full of debris. Little did I know at the time, but the whole village had been washed to sea. I was soaking wet and freezing cold. I don't know how long I was in the water. It might have been a long time. I don't know. It was getting dark outside. I could barely see the beach where our village used to be, but there was nothing left of it. I tried to move, but my leg hurt so badly and I was so cold that I couldn't move. I started screaming for help. Soon I could hear someone yelling back to me.

"Who are you?" the voice asked.

I told him who it was and then he ran away up the hill to find someone to help.

The time after the voice in the darkness left was the scariest time for me. I was alone in the water, freezing cold, hurt, and frightened. I didn't know how long it would be until he would return, or if he'd return at all. Perhaps he would get busy helping other people and forget about me. I hadn't actually seen the tsunami, so I didn't even know what had happened. One minute I was in my house and the next thing I know I was floating on the sea. From where I was, I could hear people crying, screaming, and calling out for help or to one another. Entire families were searching for one another. Parents were looking for their children and children were crying for their parents. It was all very sad and terrible.

As the waves rocked my floating island of debris, I held on tight and tried to paddle towards shore with one hand, but it was useless. I was so cold I didn't think I was going to make it.

Finally, a boat that had been out fishing or hunting—I think they had been out seal hunting—came in and saw me floating in the bay. I think it was called the Marpet. They pushed through all the floating debris and fished me out of the water. They put three sleeping bags on me, but that didn't help. They told me later that I stopped breathing for five minutes, but that I eventually came to. I don't remember anything about that, but it must be true.

Later, I learned that my mother, Anna Vlasoff, had been washed out to sea when the first wave hit. My last memory is of her running around outside her house trying to find someone to help me.

I'll never forget that.

It's been forty years since that tragic night, and in all that time, I've never gone back to Chenega. I just don't think I could stand to see where my home used to be, where my mother last stood, where my entire village was swept off the face of the earth.

Steve Eleshansky, Jr.

The End of Days

I WAS FIVE YEARS OLD on March 27, 1964. I remember that day began with my mother telling me to stay inside the house. "It's a big day today," she said, referring to Good Friday. But I didn't want to sit inside the house all day, so I kept bugging her, crying and whining to let me go outside. Finally, I wore her down and she agreed to let me go.

"Okay," she said. "But you stay close to the house. We're going to church soon."

I went down to the beach to skip rocks on the water. Little by little, I worked my way around the point below my grandfather's place. It was there that I ran into some of my cousins, Jack, Jr., Archie, Richey, and two others who I can't remember now. We started throwing rocks at cans and things. We were pretty good. A bird flew overhead, and we all threw rocks at it. Wouldn't you know that all four rocks hit that bird at the same time! We started yelling and hollering as if we had won a prize or something. Just as the bird hit the earth, the ground started shaking tremendously. I was really scared.

I thought God was mad at us for killing that bird.

When the earthquake was finally over, my uncle, Jack Kompkoff, Sr., came down to the beach from out of nowhere to pick us up. He was carrying me and some of the other kids in his arms and on his shoulders. On the way up the hill he dropped me and turned around. He had this really strange, confused look on his face. I'll never forget it. He must have seen the tide go way out all of a sudden and the first giant wave coming in. I'm sure he knew he had a quick decision to make: whether to carry the other kids up the hill first and come back for me, or to try to carry us all at one time, which would slow him down.

He chose to leave me behind and to come back for me.

I didn't know what to do. I was too young to know better. All I knew was that I didn't want to be left behind. So I stood there, just above the beach, looking around, crying, and waiting. I remember the water started rising and the boats started moving in towards me. Then big boulders started bouncing, and trees were shaking violently and some were falling over. The tree above me started falling, and then it snapped in two, about half way up, and the whole top half crashed to the ground near me. It was all so frightening.

Uncle Jack still hadn't come back for me.

Then I heard a voice yelling to me from above. It was saying, "Boy! Boy! Come up here!" I thought it was God. I thought he was really mad at me. But it was John Brizgaloff. He was calling to me from atop the bulkhead, which had slippery, moss-covered stairs leading up to it. I started towards him by crawling up the stairs on my hands and knees. The stairs were shaking, and I was sure I was going to fall. When I was at the top, John grabbed me, held me close in his arms, and spoke to me to calm me down as he quickly walked up the hill, through the village graveyard, towards the schoolhouse.

From atop his shoulders, I could see everything happening around me. Below me, I saw entire houses swallowed as the earth opened up to eat them. I could hear the sound of wood snapping and glass breaking as houses slid into the cracks, vanishing into the ground. I could see people running away from the waterfront. Behind them, I saw a giant tidal wave, a wall of water almost a hundred feet tall. It was coming in fast. From where I was, the people looked like little ants compared to the wave. I saw our house vanish under the first wave.

By this time, we were through the graveyard, and my uncle put me down so that I could climb up towards a clearing behind the schoolhouse. There were other people up there, all out of breath from running away from the wave. We all hugged quietly, without talking, because we knew how bad this was going to be for all of us. We started a fire and tried to dry out our wet socks and shoes by holding them on sticks over the fire, the way we sometimes roasted seal meat.

After a couple hours, some of us went down to the school. There were other people there, including my mother. She was all black and blue and covered in an Army blanket. She had been caught in a tidal wave, the force of which tore away all of her clothes and washed her up into a snow bank near the schoolhouse. I asked if she was all right. She said she was cold but was feeling better. I told her I was fine, that John Brizgaloff had helped me. Then I asked about my dad and my sister, Rhonda. She said they were in the house when she went looking for me. I must have had a sad look on my face because she asked why I was worried about them, and I had to tell her.

"Mom," I said sadly, trying not to cry. "I saw our house go under the water."

That's when she broke down crying because she knew that my father and baby sister had been inside the house.

I went outside for a while, trying to understand what had just happened. That's when I realized that my mom and I would be alone from then on. That it was the end of the way things had been before.

We were eventually airlifted to a hospital in Cordova. Afterwards, we were all moved to Tatitlek, where we lived in green Army tents for a long time until the government built homes for us.

1. Tatitlek, Alaska, ca. 1947

Larry M. Evanoff
On Hearing the News

I WAS THIRTEEN YEARS OLD in 1963, when I attended my first year at Wrangell Boarding School. Lots of native children went to such schools back then. Some got to stay in Alaska; others were sent far, far away. I remember I had to repeat eighth grade because I had missed so much school the year before. My father wanted me to grow up knowing some of his traditions, so he taught me how to hunt and fish and trap. He wanted me to know how to live off the land, so he took me with him.

I was fourteen years old in 1964. I was at Wrangell when the bad news arrived the day after the earthquake and tsunami. I'll never forget that day. The principal summoned me to his office and told me the bad news. He told me that my mother and father were gone. He told me the whole village was gone and lots of people with it.

I had never been in a large earthquake before, and I had never even heard of a tsunami, so I didn't believe him. What's more, I had just that day received a care package from home full of baked goods, which my mom sent to me from time to time.

"Since I had just received a package from my parents," I rationalized, "how could they be gone?"

It must have been around three o'clock in the afternoon when my aunt and sister called me to tell me what had happened to Chenega. Although they lived in Cordova at the time, the news had traveled fast. I remember picking up the black phone and the first thing they said was, "We have some really bad news." They told me, as best they could, what had happened. The told me both my parents were lost. They said

Uncle Jack, Aunt Nellie, Umma (my grandmother), Joann, and many others were gone. We talked for almost an hour.

I wanted to go home, but my aunt and sister persuaded me to stay and finish the school year. They said there was nothing I could do anyhow. They were probably right, but I still wanted desperately to go home.

Instead of going to my classes, I spent the next several days in the nurse's office crying, then sleeping, and then crying some more. I felt very alone. Finally, on the third day, the principal grabbed me and told me that I had grieved long enough. He told me to snap out of it; life goes on.

I was miserable during the rest of the school year. The school staff and teachers were supportive, but the students were curious about what had happened. They often asked me questions such as, "Are your parents dead? How did they die? Where's Chenega? How many people were killed?" All these questions just brought back my sad feelings. For the rest of that 1964 school year, my friends tried to help me a great deal.

It wasn't until summer vacation that I flew in to Cordova. It was then that I learned why my aunt and sister wanted me to stay at Wrangell. They were afraid that if I left school I would not return to finish my education. Maybe they were right, but I still have hard feelings about that, even though I know they had my best interests in mind.

It was later that I learned some of the details of that tragic day. I learned that my parents and others had run into the church for safety, but that the church was destroyed by the tidal waves, the same waves that washed away my village, my home.

My mother and father were never found.

It's been forty years since that spring and summer, but those days will stick in my mind forever. Even today, when I think back on it all, I am sad. I start crying. Just writing this down has brought back those hard feelings.

Bill Hjort
Russian Orthodox Celebrations

I GREW UP IN CHENEGA a long time before the earthquake. In those days, early spring was a happy time. Everyone was busy preparing for Easter celebrations. In many ways, the small Russian Orthodox Church was the center of life in the old village. The women worked together cleaning and decorating the church, while the men would haul skiff loads of gravel from a local beach. The gravel was carried in buckets and dumped around the church grounds. It seemed like everyone was doing something for Easter. My aunt, Sally Evanoff, was especially talented at making colorful flowers from crepe paper. They were used to decorate the interior of the church.

2. Russian Orthodox Church, 1945

3. Chenega Village, west

Our lives—the routines of our lives—were pretty much defined by the seasons.

In late April or May, usually after Easter, families would begin seal hunting, beachcombing, and collecting wild bird eggs. This was before the busy summer fishing season. Everyone really looked forward to it. It was like a big camping trip. Families would pack all their gear including bedding, tents, rifles, pots and pans. They'd go for a week or two to collect foods other than salmon, which weren't available yet. My family went seal hunting at Icy Bay, maybe five miles across from Chenega.

I remember around spring was when herring came near the village to spawn. There would be millions of them near shore in giant, swirling schools. You could actually see them splashing around on the surface. Sometimes the water would turn milky white from all their spawning. It was really amazing. There were so many. We'd just scoop them up with long nets. Grandma would cut their head off, gut them, and fry them until they were crisp. They were pretty bony and oily, but we liked them. My favorite was the females, because they had all the tiny eggs in them. Then, after the spawning, we'd go out and collect the fertilized eggs, which attached themselves to seaweed. That was part of our annual spring ritual.

It seems like almost everything we ate we hunted, fished, or gathered. The land really provided for us back then.

There was a lot of excitement when the whole village prepared for the summer fishing season. Families would pack up everything they would need for a couple months at summer fish camp, usually at Shipyard. Every family had their own special place. They set up tents or they had small trapper cabins, usually with some sort of smokehouse and steam bath. Everyone had a steam bath; it was a central part of our daily life. The old village was pretty empty during the summer.

Our village had about eight seine boats and a few other boats that were provided by the Copper River Packing Company. We'd use them to catch salmon for the company, delivering our catch every night on a daily basis. They weren't big boats. They'd carry maybe two or three tons at most. No matter where we went to catch the salmon, we had to make our delivery every night, so we didn't travel too far. I remember each boat had four bunks for sleeping, but no head. You'd have to go to the back of the boat to do your business. It was so different back then. Everything was done by hand. The boats didn't have power tools like a winch or power block until around 1958. We'd drive around looking for signs of salmon. When we found them, we'd drop our round haul nets and drag in the fish. My first trip as a young boy was with my Uncle Eddie. I learned everything about fishing from him. He was a good man.

The crew was always men. Women didn't catch salmon. I think my mother was an exception. She went with my father.

4. Chenega Village, east

In late summer and early fall, we'd catch salmon for our families. Entire families would work together drying and smoking fish for winter, each family putting away hundreds of fish. The hard-smoked fish was packed in cardboard boxes, which were stored in our smokehouses because we had no refrigeration back then.

Come winter, things settled down in the village. The kids played in the snow, skiing, sledding, and ice-skating. We put sealskin on the bottom of our skis, which made them go really fast. I remember setting traps in the woods, occasionally catching weasel or ermine. We'd watch a movie once a week up at the schoolhouse. The mail boat came by about every two weeks, weather permitting. The mailman sold things like candy and soda pop. I'd sell him my small fur pelts for about seventy-five cents each. I think a candy bar cost only a nickel.

Russian Christmas was another time of great celebration, lasting for three days. Every family baked a bunch of pies or cakes, which were passed around as gifts. There would be a procession of women and children walking around the village holding a large symbol of a star. They would stop at every house and spin the star in front of a holy picture while singing Christmas carols. A little while later, the men of the village would do the same thing with their own star. It was after all this that the baked goods were given away.

I remember, too, that adults would toss handfuls of coins into the air for the children to gather off the floor. This was especially fun. We'd scramble around trying to see who could collect the most money.

Karen Selanoff Katelnikoff
Memories Left Behind

I WAS A FOURTEEN-YEAR-OLD freshman at Wrangell Institute when the 1964 Earthquake and tidal wave hit Cheneg. My friend Tony and I were at a movie during all that destruction. When I got back to the dorm, some of the girls asked if we had felt the tremors. We hadn't.

The next morning, Myra Allen, Larry Evanoff, and I were in science class when the school nurse took us out of class. She took us to the clinic, sat us down, and told us that there had been a big earthquake and several tsunamis. She told us that many people had lost their lives. First, she told Myra that her home village of Tatitlek was okay, that there was no major damage. Next she told me that my brother and my sister, Billy and Jeanne Selanoff, were gone. Larry's loss was the worse. He had lost many members of his family. It seemed like the list of those lost just went on and on.

I felt a great sorrow for my mother and father and for all the other people who had lost friends and loved ones.

My mother finally called three days later from Cordova, where survivors were taken after being rescued. Her voice was breaking as she told us that we had lost my brother and sister, Billy and Jeannie; my sister Shirley's son, Phil, Jr.; my Aunt Dora and her three children, Cindy, Danny, and Arvella; and my Uncle Nick and aunt Mary's two daughters, Julia and Norma.

I learned that there were to be no funerals because the giant tidal waves had swept their bodies out to sea, as if they had never existed. I was numb; my young mind couldn't grasp all that loss—the horrible

5. Chenega Village schoolhouse, before the quake

scale of all that death and destruction. I went into denial. I couldn't believe all those people were dead.

For many years, I watched my father cry. He had grown up in Chenega. My mother healed faster.

Before I left for Wrangell, I remembered telling my mother about a dream I had in which a giant brown bear walked along the shore at the water's edge, and the earth trembled. I remember that she looked at me strangely after I told her. She didn't know what to make of my dream. I also remember my parent's sadness when I left to go to school in Wrangell. My brother and sister, Peter and Betty, went to school at

Mt. Edgecumbe. I still remember how peaceful the village looked from the air the day we flew away.

Those are the only things I can remember after I talked with my mother. I completely blocked out other memories of Chenega. I couldn't recall family or village life, what the little school looked like, and the games we played, what people did for a living. I couldn't even remember anything about the people who had died. It was as if I had erased my memories as the tidal waves had erased the village.

My memories finally started coming back in my early thirties. It was like watching movie clips in the theater of my mind. I would cry and laugh when I remembered something sad or happy. There were times when I would clench my fists and cry, "O Lord! Why did you destroy our village?" Then I'd think about how my parents and all the others felt who were there during the earthquake and tidal waves.

6. A school class portrait, 1946. Left row: Ceorgie Chernoff, Arlene Totemoff, Dora Brizgaloff, Norman Selanoff. Middle row: Phillip Totemoff, Frieda Brizgaloff, Mikey Eleshansky, Wally Brizgaloff, Billy Hjort. Right row: Mischa Kompkoff, Don Kompkoff, Richard Kompkoff, Mary Ribaloff, Dora Ribaloff.

The Day That Cries Forever

After the earthquake, we were relocated to Tatitlek. Others moved to Cordova, Anchorage, or Valdez. During the summer of 1964, we lived in Army-issue tents until the Bureau of Indian Affairs (BIA) built our houses. My mother was happy because she came from Tatitlek; but my father was sad because he had lost his home. For a long time we felt like we didn't belong in our new home, but there were many people who welcomed us and tried to make us feel at home.

Life in Tatitlek was good. My father did well in the fishing industry; mother continued to be a wife and mother. After high school, my siblings married and had children of their own. Some of them moved away. I returned after being gone for seven years. Nowadays, Tatitlek is my home, but I think about moving to Chenega Bay. Maybe I will some day.

I learned one big lesson after the 1964 Good Friday Earthquake: never take life for granted. You never know what will happen today or tomorrow.

To the many people who died in Chenega on that terrible day, I love you all.

Vechnaya Pamyat. Memory eternal.

Avis Kompkoff
Premonitions of Things Yet to Come

I REMEMBER THAT GOOD FRIDAY began like any other day. The people of Chenega were going about their daily lives. Nothing foretold of the tragedy to come.

Richard Kompkoff was visiting me at the time when everything began to happen. He was just walking out the door to go home when I heard a voice telling me to send Joann up to my mom and dad's house. I don't know why I felt I had to get her out of the house. I just had this feeling. Some voice was speaking to me. I asked Joann if she wanted to go visit her grandparents, and she eagerly agreed. I called Richard back in to take her with him. Then I asked Joey if he wanted to go, too. He also agreed. But then I heard the voice again. It told me not to send him, so I told him to stay.

I had planned to take a steam bath with Margaret Borodkin. Everyone took steam baths back then. Margaret said there wasn't enough water, so I decided to take a hot bath at home in my own bathtub.

I still remember seeing Julia Kompkoff waving at me through the window. It was a pretty day outside, bright and sunny. I took my baby, Lloyd, out of the baby seat he was sitting in and slipped his little, warm booties on his feet. While I was looking around for clothes to wear after the bath, I saw Joey running to his bed, his eyes wide open like he was really scared of something.

Suddenly a great jolt went through the house and everything started shaking really bad. It was an earthquake. But it didn't end quickly like other earthquakes. It just kept going. I was worried the house would fall down on us, so I grabbed Lloyd and Joey and ran outside. I could see their dad down on the beach. He came running up and grabbed Joey, while I held on to Lloyd. Steve Eleshansky came down and stood beside us. He was holding his baby daughter. They lived above us back then.

Someone started yelling that there might be a tidal wave. He said to get up hill. I don't remember who it was, but we started to run uphill toward the woods above the village.

Steve and his baby were right behind me when the first wave came in. I was ahead of them. The wave didn't get me, but when I turned around, they were gone. I got stuck in the deep snow or in a hole or something. When I got out, I had lost my slippers. I was barefoot as I kept making my way up the mountain. When I was up high enough, I crossed over and went down a little ways to the schoolhouse. I remember the teacher gave me a pair of her boots to wear.

Then there was another big earthquake, and we knew another wave would come, so a group of us went back up the mountain where it would be safe. We stayed up there all night standing around a big campfire. I don't know how I knew it at the time, but somehow I knew that my mom and dad and Joann didn't make it. I just knew it in my heart. Later, we learned that many people didn't make it. Some people were never found. Joann was found two weeks later, washed ashore at Knight's Island.

The next morning a Coast Guard airplane flew overhead and reported that everything was all right. But Jim Osborn, who delivered our mail, flew by and saw that everything was not all right. He flew some of us to Cordova.

Almost ten years later, in 1974 or 1975, I was asked to fly out to the old village with some lawyers. It seems that the government didn't quite believe that anyone had ever lived in Chenega since there was nothing left but the old schoolhouse on the little hill. I spent the day there, walking around pointing out where everyone had lived, where each house had been. I told them stories about life in Chenega.

A few days later, we had a meeting with the lawyers and Hollis Hendricks. After some discussion, the lawyers agreed that Chenega had

Premonitions of Things Yet to Come

been an established community and agreed that we could relocate and build a new village. I remember Nick Kompkoff telling me that if it weren't for me going with those lawyers, we wouldn't have a new village site at Chenega Bay.

〰️
〰️

7. Aerial view of Chenega Village following the quake

Carol Ann Kompkoff
The Longest Night

I WAS WALKING with my two sisters to the outhouse at the end of the dock when the earthquake struck. It was a very scary experience. I remember it clearly. The whole dock was moving back and forth. My ten-year-old sister, Julia, told us to go back. We saw our father, Nicholas Kompkoff, running down to the beach to look for our three older brothers. He learned that the boys were with their godfather. We called him Big Daddy. When the ground finally stopped shaking, the water went out of the bay. The whole bay was empty! When the first giant wave was coming in, my father grabbed my three-year-old sister, Norma Jean, and me and told Julia to follow him and to run as fast as she could.

The wave caught Julia as it was going out, and when my father reached out to grab her, he lost hold of Norma. I remember seeing my godmother, Anna Vlasoff, standing in the doorway of her house, which was floating by. She was calling to my father in Segcestun—our native language. When I was ten, I learned that she was telling my father to hand me to her. She knew my sisters were already gone.

Only my father and I made it up the hill near the school, where a light pole fell on him and hurt his back, and he lost hold of me as well. My uncle, Henry Selanoff, and Mike Eleshansky pulled me out of the water from atop a snow bank behind the church. I was wearing a hooded jacket. They grabbed the hood to pull me out of the water. The zipper always stuck, which was good this time because I didn't fall through. That jacket saved my life! My mother always hated that jacket because of the bad zipper, but she certainly liked it after it saved me.

The Longest Night

It was awful. I was wet and cold and crying while walking around looking for my mother. Everyone up at the school was crying. People were looking for their lost children and other family members. Many of them were never found. I remember there was a bonfire and people sitting around or standing comforting each other. Miss Madsen, the schoolteacher, was handing out clothes and shoes to those who needed them.

Sometime during the long night, a woman's voice could be heard crying out for help. My godfather, Mark Selanoff, and some other men who had been out hunting on his boat rescued a girl. It turned out to be Margaret Borodkin, my god-sister, who I last saw in my godmother's house as it was washed out to sea.

I don't remember anything about the other waves. It was dark and everything happened so fast. I must have been too busy trying to survive the first one.

The next day an airplane flew overhead and kept going. Apparently, the pilot was unfamiliar with Chenega, and when he saw a bunch of people standing outside the schoolhouse waving, he thought everything was okay. He didn't realize that the entire village had been destroyed.

Fortunately, a pilot who had heard on the news that the epicenter was close to Chenega, flew out to Chenega Island, saw the devastation, and reported the news to the Red Cross. It wasn't long before help arrived.

Donald P. Kompkoff, Sr.
The Long Road Ahead

I was living in Valdez on March 27, 1964. My friend, Darwin Barrie, and I had returned from Dutch Harbor the week before. We went down to the dock to work on the Chena, a long shore ship. We had lost our union cards, which meant we couldn't work that day. Because we had missed working on two ships, two other longshoremen took our place.

We climbed into my car, a little Austin Healy Sprite, and drove to my dad's house, which was only a few blocks from the dock. The earthquake began a few minutes after we arrived. I ran to the oil stove to shut it off (so it wouldn't start a fire), and then I ran for the door. Everything was shaking so hard we could hardly stand up. We were bumping into both sides of the porch, and the water was rising above our ankles.

Outside, telephone and light poles were falling down, and sparks were flying everywhere. We went next door to Darwin's sister's house to check on her. Her name was Jean McCoy. Neither she nor her two daughters were home, so we climbed back into the car and went looking for them. We found them a few blocks away. We drove back to her house to pick up Jean's son, Bucky, who had the mumps. We all piled into the car and headed out of town. As I was driving, the road ahead would open up and water would shoot up from the crack, maybe fifteen or twenty feet high. This happened to us maybe three or four times. We had to stop each time and wait.

We drove out about ten miles to where a lot of the townspeople were gathered. We stayed there until the police told us it was safe to return. It must have been around 8:30 P.M. by then. About an hour later, a huge gas tank blew up, so we had to evacuate to Copper Center.

The next day, I got the bad news that the tidal waves had washed away my village. I made phone call after phone call and learned that the survivors of Chenega were being evacuated to Cordova in planes and two boats, the Marpet and the Gypsy Queen. I heard that my mom and dad were at their fish camp on Axel Lind Island. I also learned that my brother, Joe, had lost his daughter, Joann, and that my brother, Nick, had lost two girls, Norma and Julia Ann. Twenty-six people perished in Chenega (three were on Nellie Juan Island). I flew to Cordova to see my parents and my brothers. I was so relieved to see them, but it was so sad.

Eventually, the village of Chenega was relocated to Tatitlek. We lived in tents for the summer. By fall, the BIA had built homes for every family. But not all families stayed in Tatitlek. Some moved to Anchorage, Cordova, or Valdez.

It was so hard to see all of the people hurting from the disaster. It still is. Time may have dulled the pain, but the pain is still there. Even today, just to speak of the earthquake and tidal waves brings tears to the eyes of many of my relatives. It's such a hurtful memory. It's like wanting to take the pain away from a sick child.

But you can't.

It will never go away.

Mary Ann Kompkoff

The Calm before the Storm

THE MORNING OF March 27, 1964, was calm and gray. There was no wind and no rain. It was strangely silent. Even nature was quiet. There weren't even sounds from birds or anything. Maybe they knew something bad was about to happen.

Around five o'clock that evening I was cleaning the house. There was supposed to be a movie that night. I had a pot of chili simmering on the stove. I decided to go see my sister, Dora, so I turned down the stove real low and went to visit her. She was ironing her curtains when I walked into her house. It was during Lent. She looked sad. She probably had a feeling of some kind.

I asked if I could see the baby, and she said she was sleeping, but she told me to go ahead and wake her up so that she wouldn't be too tired when we went to see the movie. I decided to let her sleep some more while I sat down and watched Dora. She was ironing really slowly. She was really sad about it.

I remember she said, "I don't even know why I'm doing this."

The effect of her words didn't dawn on me until long after the earthquake. It was as if she knew something terrible was about to happen.

I left her house to go home. I don't remember seeing anyone else. On the way, I decided to go and visit Shirley (Totemoff). She wasn't doing anything. She was just sitting around waiting for the movie to begin. I didn't stay there long. On my way back home, I saw my husband, Nick Kompkoff. He was on his way to the little pool hall to play pool. We used to have a little pool hall. All of a sudden a tremendous rumbling began, and the ground started shaking violently. I told him to go get the girls. Shirley's husband, Phil Totemoff, came and told Shirley and me to get out of the house. I don't remember where he came from, but he told us to run up the hill.

I was at Shirley's house during the whole earthquake, but we ran, after Philip's warning. I saw the second wave just after we ran out of Shirley's house. I saw the village going out with the wave—on it, in it. Everything was being carried out with the wave. We were heading up to higher ground when we ran into John and Alice Vlasoff. John yelled, "Don't look back! Just keep running up higher! We were running through deep snow. We kept falling in the snow, which slowed us down.

When the third wave hit, I looked back, and I saw my brother-in-law, Steve Eleshansky. He was holding his baby, Rhonda. I saw June Eleshansky with her babies in both her arms. They were trying to get up hill, but the third wave caught them. They didn't have time. I saw all this. But then John Vlasoff told us, "Keep going! Keep going! Don't panic. Just keep going and don't look back." So we kept running up the hill.

We thought we were the only ones left.

Then we started hearing voices. I didn't know where they were coming from, but I could hear people calling out to one another. We could hear someone yelling from out in the bay, but there was nothing any one of us could do. We couldn't go down there to reach her. It was Margaret Borodkin. She was hanging on to some lumber floating in all that debris. My brother, Marky, was out hunting with Nick Eleshansky. They were just coming home. It was shortly after the waves had struck, and they couldn't get into the bay because of all the debris floating around out there. They heard Margaret. They're the ones who took her out of the water, put her in the boat, and kept her warm.

I didn't know where my three girls were. I didn't know where my youngest son was. My two older ones were with me. As we got up to higher ground, where everyone was going from the other side of the village, we met up with them. We were so happy to find each other. After a while, we decided to go back down the hill a little ways, to the schoolhouse, because it wasn't destroyed. It would be warm there.

When I got there, I saw my sister wrapped in a blanket. She was so cold, and she was probably in shock. I thought she was drunk. I didn't even go near her. Kenny Vlasoff and my husband heard some one calling. It was a lady's voice. They went down toward the voice and saw it was Aunt Tiny. She was stuck in the snow with not a stitch of clothes on—just one sock. She had been caught by all three waves. She was really cold and bruised up pretty bad. They picked her up and took her to the schoolhouse. That's where they had to keep her because nobody could carry her up the hill until the next day.

There were so many aftershocks and some of them were really strong. It was like they weren't going to stop, so the men decided that the women and children should go up to higher ground just in case.

Nick Kompkoff, Jr.
A Force of Nature

I WAS NINE YEARS OLD on that sunny day in March of 1964. I was down on the beach playing with Mark and Jerry Selanoff. It was our favorite place to play. We went the opposite direction of a group of other boys. We had gone down on the beach to the right of the village, while Paul, Billy, George—I can't remember who else was with them—had gone down the beach to the left of the village. We were out there for a while, but then we came back to Aunt Shirley's house to get some water to drink. My mom was visiting Aunt Shirley. My dad, Nick Kompkoff, Sr., was at the pool hall. We were in the house, when all of a sudden it started shaking, and the front door got jammed and it wouldn't open. Shirley's husband, Phillip Totemoff, had to bust the door open so we could get out of there. He was yelling at us to run up the hill.

In the distance, I could hear someone calling for help. Phil went to help whoever it was. He was one of the bravest men I ever knew. I always respected him for that. Men were like that back then. They were like heroes. They were always helping everybody. I never saw my father cry except, many years later, when he talked about Chenega and all the people who were lost in the tsunami.

The ground was shaking so hard that it was difficult to walk or run. All around me the houses were rocking from side to side really bad, and the ground was actually heaving, waving up and down. I had never seen anything like it. My dad ran home to turn off the gas to our stove. He was probably worried that the line would break and burn down the house.

I looked down toward the bay, and I could see my three sisters on the dock, which was fluttering like a ribbon. All over the village some people were standing around not knowing what to do, while others were running around yelling and screaming. I couldn't make out what they were saying. I saw some people running back toward their house. I guess they thought they'd be safe there. Some of them never came out.

Everything was happening so fast.

It was then that the waves started coming in. It wasn't like you'd think. The first wave wasn't like a giant cresting wave or anything. It wasn't like in a movie or something. It was more like a fast, rising tide. I remember the water was really dirty. It must have been from the force of the water churning up the sea floor and from scraping dirt from the earth once it hit land.

It was really loud, too. I was scared. I ran for a ways and then got stuck in deep snow. The snow was maybe waist deep and crusted over on top. I kept breaking through, which slowed me down.

My dad ran down to the dock to fetch my sisters. My oldest sister, who was running ahead of him, was pushed forward by the surging tide. When the tide went back out, she was carried past my father, who already had my second-oldest and youngest sisters in his arms. When he reached out to grab her, he accidentally let go of my second-oldest sister and missed my oldest sister as she washed by. My dad barely had my youngest sister by the hood of her jacket.

Almost as fast as it came in, the water receded, going way out. Then, a little bit later, the second wave struck. It was more like a giant, breaking tidal wave. It smashed everything in its path, tearing houses apart like a giant bulldozer made of seawater. Our house was down by the old cemetery. It was destroyed like all the other houses in the village. The third wave came in and cleaned up the destruction, washing everything out to sea.

One thing that amazed me, the thing I'll never forget, is how much debris there was floating in the bay after the waves. The whole bay was just a jumbled mess of floating debris from the lumber of houses, warehouses and sheds, the church, boats, and furniture.

Everything that used to be our village was out there. But the next morning, the bay was clean and flat and calm. The surface was like a mirror. I don't know what happened to all the debris. Sometimes I think maybe a giant crack opened up in the sea floor and swallowed everything, or maybe the tide just carried it all away.

It was so clean, in fact, that when the Coast Guard first flew over Chenega, they reported that the village was okay because they didn't see any signs of disaster. No one outside knew what had happened until the mailman, who knew what the village should look like, flew over and reported that all the houses and buildings were gone.

I eventually made it up the hill above the schoolhouse. Other people were there, too. We were all cold, so the men gathered wood and built a big fire. For a long time we all just huddled around it to keep warm. I remember my mom crying.

Later, someone said we should go down to the schoolhouse. Other people were gathered there. I saw my Aunt Dorothy. We called her Aunt Tiny. She acted like she was drunk or something, but I think it was because she was spun around and around in the tidal waves. I think she was really dizzy and disoriented and cold. She had lost her husband and daughter. Mrs. Totemoff lost her oldest son. My cousin, Billy Selanoff, who had been down on the beach, was gone. Lots of people didn't make it. It seemed like everyone lost someone in his or her family. They never found most of the bodies. It was all really sad.

It still is sad.

We were relocated to Tatitlek after that. We stayed there for three years until we moved to Anchorage in 1967. In my sophomore year of high school, I wrote a story about that day. I don't remember what happened to it. I tried to write about it again while I was in the Army.

It's a hard thing to talk about.

Paul Kompkoff, Jr.
The Short-Lived Days of Summer

CHENEGA WAS a wonderful place to live before the 1964 Alaska Earthquake. I remember the joy of going to Shipyard every summer to catch fish. Whole families went. It was a busy time. I remember my dad and uncles teaching me everything about fishing.

They were peaceful, happy times.

We moved to Cordova before the earthquake. It was hard for me there. I had a hard time trying to fit in. People were always in a hurry to do things, but they never seemed to get them done. Life in Chenega had been simpler, slower.

I remember the day of the earthquake. I was walking home from the store with my sisters, Sharon and Sue. All of a sudden, the road

8. Cooperative store

started moving. Everything was shaking and moving. Trees were shaking back and forth. My sisters held on to each other, but they were knocked off their feet. I tried to help them up, but I fell down, too. I remember the earthquake lasted for a long time. It was really something.

When it was over, we ran home. We were worried about our family. My mother had been deep-frying homemade donuts when the earthquake hit, and the oil splashed all over and caught fire. Luckily, she was able to put it out before it burned down the house. My father was out seal hunting at the time. We were worried about him. His boat got stuck out on the mudflats when the tide went out, and he didn't get home until late. We were glad when he came home.

Later, we heard what had happened to Chenega.

Our home was gone.

Everything was gone.

9. The dock, viewed from the store

Pete Kompkoff, Jr.
Chenega Days

THERE WERE ABOUT a hundred people living in Chenega before the earthquake. Maybe a little more. I remember that there was no running water or electricity when I was a boy. We had to pack water, and we only had outhouses. Everything we did was through subsistence. Of course, we had some staples that came in on the mail boat. But for the most part, the village was self-sustaining; it had its own culture, its own means and ways of providing for families. Each family did their own thing. They went out hunting and fishing for food. Whenever there was an abundance of food, it was shared with the rest of the community. No one was left out. People shared with one another. It was a community.

Back then, the young and the middle-aged people—as well as the older ones—went hunting. They would go out fishing or hunting for deer or goat, seal, sea lion, or porpoise; they even hunted grouse and ducks—whatever they could harvest to feed their families. Throughout the course of the year, the seasons told us what to do, how to live off the land. It was a lifestyle very unlike city life, for sure, because it was a life that was born for the village.

We had visitors that came to the village, not a lot, but sometimes writers and photographers, and we had a mail boat that came in on a monthly basis. Maybe it was every two weeks the mail boat came in from Cordova. I think it was called the Sirus or Siren. I remember you could go aboard and they'd have a table full of candy. You could smell the aroma of sweets. I would always go down to the boat with my dad. It was such a treat for me to go along because the skipper would call

Chenega Days

10 & 11. Chenega Bend across the seasons

out, "How you doing, partner?" and he'd give me a candy bar. I remember it was a Snickers chocolate bar. Oh my goodness, it was just so good.

It was a pretty normal village for back then. There were happy times and sad times. There was alcohol-related violence, just as there is in villages today. In such a small community, people had to learn how to cope with one another. But in the normal course of life, it wasn't that bad. It was a special place to grow up.

Each family sustained a subsistence lifestyle in Chenega. Each family member would be part of a hunting party, hunting seal for instance, or they would fish for salmon or crab, or collect shellfish when the tide was out. Nature provided everything. The land and the people were intermingled.

I remember that when I first started going to school I didn't speak English. I didn't know any English. That was pretty common back then. It was forbidden for us to speak Alutiiq at school. We couldn't speak our own language. It was an ordeal. During my first six years of education in Chenega, our teachers were the Polings, Mr. and Mrs. John Poling. They had two sons, Don and Mitch. Don became one of our god-brothers. I remember we used to go out in these old canoes or just play along the beach. Back then there used to be big icebergs that would wash up against the beach at Chenega. I remember seeing an old photograph of us standing beside a big iceberg down near the dock.

12. Iceberg at the store dock

Another thing I remember vividly is one spring, maybe it was early summer, I remember there used to be these long steps that went up the hill to the school. I had a pack of matches in my pocket, and I lit the dry grass on fire alongside the steps, and Holy Macaroni! The whole hillside caught on fire and it was going up towards the school! Next thing you know, all the men from the village were up on that hillside trying to trample out the fire. I just ran away and hid. Luckily, they stopped it before it got to the school.

I remember how every summer the whole village used to take off and go fishing at Nellie Juan. It might have been around early or mid May. Instead of having a camp set up right next to everyone else from the village, my dad made a deal with someone to get some property with a small cabin on it around the corner from Shipyard. Everyone else was around the corner in a little bay. I think my father traded an outboard motor and skiff for the land. He made some kind of trade. Anyway, we got that property and it's been our property for years.

All the families used to go there. There were all these NJ boats—NJ stands for Nellie Juan—which were fishing boats the cannery would provide for all the male members that were qualified to fish. Each boat would take a four-man crew. There was a captain for every boat. There must have been ten captains, and they were heads of families. My father was one of them, my godfather was one, Willy Evanoff, William Kompkoff, Jack Kompkoff; the list goes on. It was something that everybody in Chenega did during the fishing season. We'd spend the whole summer there.

There was the cannery, a company store, and the store would allow everyone from Chenega to have credit. Even if it was a poor fishing season and there wasn't a profit, the company would allow us credit so that we could buy groceries, flour—all the goods we needed to last us through the winter. When the next summer's fishing season began, we'd already have a bill, so we had to go back and work for them to pay off our bill.

Sometimes we'd take off for Cordova for clam digging. Cordova was the razor-clam capitol of the world. That's what they used to say. The cannery would put us up in small cabins over in Whiteshed. All of

13. A Nellie Juan boat

our families would go out and dig clams. Razor clams were so plentiful back then. I remember Paul Kompkoff. I think his family produced the most, along with Phil Totemoff. We were always competitive, always trying to see who could get the most clams.

One time we came back to town from Whiteshed and it was high tide, so we couldn't dig clams. I took my dad's skiff out and raced around with some of the other guys. We were racing around, and when I turned hard, the flat-bottomed skiff slid into the wake of another boat so hard that the motor came off the back of Dad's boat. I was leaning over the stern holding onto the handle of the forty-horse Johnson, and it's still running and I'm trying to hang onto it and shut it off at the same time. I finally managed to lift it out of the water and pull it aboard. By that time it quit running. The carburetor and cylinders must have been full of saltwater. One of the other guys towed me into the harbor, and I took the motor up to the outboard shop. They worked on it and got it running again, which was a good thing because I had to have it back on the boat and running before my dad went to work in the morning. My dad never did find out.

Those are some of the good memories of my life and experiences in Chenega before the earthquake and the tidal waves.

Back then we had summer camps all around Prince William Sound. We had summer camps at Piget Point, Applegate Island, Nellie Juan, and Port Wells. In the early part of the season, we used to go up to Port Wells, and my dad would climb over the hill and go over to all the college glaciers—those glaciers named after universities. We used to go with two other families, the Evanoffs and Eleshanskys.

My dad was a hunter, trapper, fisherman, and carpenter. You had to be a jack-of-all-trades in such a small community. Those are the things I remember most about him. My mother was a great cook and a great conversationalist. One Christmas in Tatitlek, my mother baked twenty-six pies in one day. It was an amazing thing.

Henry Makarka

The Long Summer of Clams

I WAS IN CORDOVA when it happened. We were sitting down to supper around six o'clock or near that time. We were all sitting around the table, my wife and six children, and we were just about to say a prayer and eat when suddenly the sound of a rumbling roar began. We immediately began to wonder what was going on and then a violent shaking began, and we all recognized that it was an earthquake.

We opened the door and one of the children went into the bathroom and held the hot water tank to keep it from tipping over. We looked out the door and the electric wires were snapping and sparks were flying, and the whole earth was like an ocean. I looked up to the mountain range and it looked as though it was an ocean. The hills were rolling just like waves on the ocean. We were stunned and wondered what we should do, but we just remained in the house looking out while the earth was shaking.

It lasted for quite a while. I don't remember exactly how long. And then it stopped as suddenly as it had come, and everyone was wondering what we should do. Then the tsunami warnings started coming out on the radio, warning us to go to higher ground. So we left everything in the house and packed up a few items, snack foods mostly, and hiked up the hill. The whole town was going up to the hills up towards Mt. Eyak. People were really concerned about one another, asking each other if we were all okay and if we had all our families. It was really quite an experience because it didn't matter who you were—rich man, poor man, beggar, thief, doctor, lawyer, merchant, fisherman—they were all climbing up the hill, and we were all concerned about each other.

That was mighty fine. But everybody was scared; everybody was frightened.

The aftershocks were tremendous. I looked out at the bay and the tide was rushing in like a river. The tide was coming in and out several times within a couple of hours. The docks and the boats and the warehouses on the waterfront were all resting in and out, up and down, with the tide.

That night, we all huddled around different houses that were up on the hill. On the next morning we went back home, everybody was going back home who dared to go home. It was really frightening. It really was something.

Before the earthquake, Cordova was considered a friendly town, and the people were usually friendly. But shortly after the earthquake, it wasn't too long before greed and selfishness came to the people with a "good for me" and "hell with you" attitude. It was as if the feelings of concern and compassion we had for each other up on the hill were gone. Greed had come to the people. It was a sad situation.

That earthquake really changed the subsistence patterns of the area. Before the earthquake, Cordova had been the clam capital of Alaska. But the violent shifting and shaking of the earth changed the depth of the bay by at least six feet, leaving miles and miles of clam beds high and dry—no longer covered by high tides.

That summer, tourists came in and walked around Main Street saying how beautiful the town was, but it sure did stink. That's what they said. Well, naturally it would. Within a couple of weeks, all those exposed waterfront clam beds were dying and rotting in the hot summer sun. You could walk around on the mudflats picking up tons of butter clams, cockles, horse clams; they were all dead on the surface or just beneath it. They were rotting, and when the west wind blew, it blew that stench of rotting clams right into town. It was hilarious at the time, but it was sad as far as the subsistence lifestyle. We used to say that when the tide was out, the table was set because all you had to do was walk around on the beaches and collect food to eat. But that was all gone. The razor clam beds throughout the whole area were killed off. In the time after that, there were hardly any clams at all. No butter clams, no cockles. Things were pretty scarce as far as subsistence goes. It took quite a while before people came back to their normal selves.

A lot of the native people were concerned for their relatives in the Sound and at the village of Chenega, Tatitlek, Valdez, Seward, and Whittier. We were all listening to the news and wondering how they were because of the massive tidal wave that destroyed Valdez and Chenega. We also heard the news about Anchorage, how the whole downtown Fourth Avenue area had collapsed, destroying a lot of buildings. A lot of people were concerned about the people in Chenega because that's near where the epicenter of the earthquake was, right in that area. A lot of natives were concerned about their relatives who had lived there.

Andy Selanoff
Villagers without a Village

"I thank thee for the heritage of those that fear thy name."
—Psalms

I WAS BORN the eldest son of Mary Popoff and John Selanoff. Brother to Nick and Norman Selanoff. According to census records, I was born near Fairmont Island in Prince William Sound, sometime in the summer of 1927. I married Julia Ford in Kenai, Alaska, in 1968. I have four children, two girls and two boys. I have six grandchildren, of which two boys are adopted through marriage.

My Grandma was very good with the needle and thread. She made thread out of porpoise sinew for putting together the sealskin covering on the bidarka frame. Grandpa Black Stephen was very good in woodcarving. He carved ulus and soupspoons. He was one of the best bidarka frame builders in Chenega.

14. Bidarka construction shop

The Day That Cries Forever

15. A fully loaded, sea-going bidarka (Willy Evanoff)

When I was younger, elders respected everything around them and what they believed in. Nothing was taken from the land without genuine respect, because it meant survival. Back then a hunter would never butcher a seal in the same place it was shot. It would be taken to a different place to be butchered. This was done so the next seal that came along could use the same spot because it was clean. The same method was done in the bear den, so that another bear could use it to hibernate. These locations were marked in memory, year after year and time after time. The need to survive formed a family, and a family formed a community, and a village was born.

The Chief of the village was vested with power by the people and for the people. He was very much involved with the village families, especially when two young people felt they were chosen for each other. I remember an elder once passed this example on to me: "I went to the Chief in Chenega to ask about marrying this girl. I went by myself because I had been orphaned and I had no one to help me in this matter. In his wisdom, the Chief said 'no.' I went ahead and married this girl anyway. Our marriage lasted one month!"

Villagers without a Village

The same elder once told me of another incident about the wisdom of the Chief: "Mr. Hanley had finished construction on a cannery and went to Chenega to meet with the Chief and the men of the village. Mr. Hanley said to the Chief, 'I need one man I can teach how to round haul salmon on 20ft. double-enders in shallow water.' The chief replied, 'No, you will have to teach all the men.'" Mr. Hanley agreed to take all the men from the village. Because of the Chief's wisdom, one of the largest tent camps in Prince William Sound was born. All the families moved to the summer camp called "Shipyard" because all the cannery equipment, pot scows, pile drivers, and gear scows were stored there for the winter.

Eventually, the Chief began to lose power over the people. The people leaned more to the new spiritual guidance that they didn't fully understand.

Poverty never hindered hospitality. My grandma and grandpa always invited their friends who brought their own teacups. Friends came for breakfast, with grandma serving tea, dried salmon, and bread on a bleached flour sack, spread on the floor as her table. Her teapot and sugar bowl consisted of an empty fruit tin can.

Life on Chenega Island was a life of survival, of living close to nature. We would trap to make cash to buy the things the land couldn't provide. Mickey Eleshansky, one of the best trappers in the village, taught me everything I know about survival. He showed me how to trap mink. We would set up deadfalls on Knights Island (Lower Herring Bay and Dryer Bay) for mink, sending the pelts off to Sears & Roebuck for $5.00 a pound. That was good money back then. I learned a lot from Mickey, and if I didn't make a kill, he never reprimanded me. He was a patient teacher of the old ways. I learned how to hunt from my father. I remember him teaching me how to paddle our bidarka in the ice flow, which was very important in the dangerous, icy cold waters.

Life in Chenega consisted of the bare necessities, and sometimes we lacked even this. Making money was seasonal. Many of the people of Chenega worked for the cannery in Nellie Juan. I remember purse seining for the cannery with the rest of the village. At the end of the fishing season, a complete a winter's supply of food was bought. Our staple foods were flour, sugar, coffee, and tea.

Our traditional way of life was unique. In the early months of winter the men would go hunting in a group. They would take a few loaves of bread, and when the lunch sack was empty they would rely on the kill. In the bottom of each survival sack was a recipe for a treat called bannock. Flour, lard, salt, baking powder, and water were mixed together making a stiff batter, which would be browned on both sides in a cast iron skillet. This recipe was probably passed on from the Russian explorers. During the spring seal hunts, it would take seven female sealskins to cover a bidarka frame. Men would sell the seal scalp for $2.00 a head.

The whole family went camping in the spring. Every family was ready for the summer season. The men went commercial fishing six days a week. After the commercial season was over, it was time to set up fish camp to dry salmon for personal use. Not every family had a fish camp. Some had their smoke houses right at home. It was during one of these events that I recall my Grandpa telling the fox farmer who was using a gill-net to catch salmon for fox feed, he told the fox farmer, "If you set that net you'll get all the fish and what will my family have to eat? I'm waiting for these salmon to go up stream. They are waiting for the flood, and you better go somewhere else." The farmer left.

I recall the years we lived together as a village were full of joy. People lived close to nature, they traveled, hunted and camped together, and no one was left out in village life. We celebrated the different Russian Orthodox holidays with what we had. People were very close to one another, sharing all that they had. No family went without in Chenega. When one family ran out of tea, the mother would send her child next door to borrow tea and bring it back to the family. People helped each other. Today the word borrow implies that a thing must be repaid. I don't know if my current neighbor would give me bread if I were out of bread. Growing up, I remember countless times that I went to borrow staple foods—bread being the most common, for without bread, we would not survive. I am very proud of my ancestors. I am proud of where I came from, even with all its hardships and the struggles that went with it.

When I think of Chenega, I remember mostly the way people shared everything and went places together. I recall the times we went over to a beach across from the village for Russian Easter picnics of native foods. A Russian Orthodox priest would come to visit once a year. I remember the Priest staying at the home of Steve Vlasoff, who was the Russian Orthodox Lay Reader at the time.

However, as I grew older, village life seemed to lose my interest; nothing in the village would sustain me. Like many young men, I had wanderlust. So, in 1957, at the age of thirty, I boarded the MS Hygiene bound for Juneau. From Juneau I went by floatplane to Sitka on a government-relocating program. I used the program to get me from Juneau to Sitka, where I found a job in the hospital at Mt. Edgecumbe boarding school.

I had to work outside Chenega to make money. That's where the jobs existed. This took me from the house I had built in Chenega to living here and there, where the employment was. I built my house with my own two hands. I bought all the lumber I needed from Columbia Wards Saw Mill in Whittier. After I left Chenega, my house became vacant for anyone who wanted to live in it. That was the way it was in Chenega—people shared everything, even their homes. So my empty house became occupied.

I never returned to Chenega to live. Little did I know at the time that I would be alienated from my native way of life. With sad realization and embarrassment after sixteen years away from my language, I thought I could converse with my first cousin, but I could not form the words that I wanted to say in my native tongue. Living outside my culture for so many years, I almost lost my native identity. Living in this American culture where we live close to shopping malls and grocery stores, we have telephones and catalogs to order anything we want. We live in a culture in which people rarely experience the deep desire of need or want. We have grown accustomed to never having to want something "real bad" because all we have to do is buy it, order it, or drive to get it. I am amazed each time I shop at the local Soldotna

Fred Meyers grocery department store. When I see all the displays of food on the shelves, I get a little emotional sometimes and ask myself, "Where was I when all this food was made? I never saw it when I was growing up."

On Good Friday in March 1964, I was thirty-six years old. I was scheduled to work on a freighter ship in Valdez, but for some reason I decided to take a plane from Valdez over to Cordova. On my time off I was spending the afternoon at the bowling alley in Cordova. I was roaming, living where I could. At the time, I was renting a room at Cordova House.

I guess the earthquake happened around 5:30 P.M. Darkness had already set in. In the dark of night, not much could be done to help bring aid to my village. I don't even recall feeling the quake. I don't recall much being done at the time of the quake. In Cordova the water level rose gradually, covering the dock of two-by-twelve planks. Cordova bridges were destroyed en route to mile 13 at the airport, and of course a segment of the Million Dollar Bridge collapsed.

I remember my first cousin, Mark Selanoff, and George Borodkin calling from Chenega on their boat. They must have used a radiotele phone onboard to call the Cordova Coast Guard. They had been on a seal-hunting trip in Icy Bay. I guess they may have been the first to see Chenega in the morning after the devastation of the tsunamis. I heard that Anna Vlasoff (Margaret Borodkin's mother) was found in the debris on Chenega Island, and two days later Mickey Eleshansky found his wife, Sally, on a beach at Knights Island. It was all very sad.

Life for the survivors of Chenega changed dramatically after that terrible day. Like everyone else, I no longer had a village community to return to. I no longer had a place to call my own. So I worked and lived between Cordova, Valdez, and Anchorage.

As result of the tsunami, the National Disaster Agency came to the relief of our people, offering to replace whatever we needed for survival, such as boats, motors, and rifles. All their hunting and fishing gear and equipment was replaced by the Agency. We were given the freedom to have the boats custom built and catalogs to order a rifle if we had lost one.

Villagers without a Village

I had my eighteen-foot boat made by the Tiedeman boys out of Cordova, because even though I was not living in Chenega at the time of the tsunami, I was qualified with the rest of the people to receive a new boat. This wooden, marine plywood boat came with a brand new twenty-five hp Johnson motor. It was the nicest boat I ever owned. With my new boat and rifle, I set off the following spring making my way through the Sound. I went the route of Unakwik to Ester Pass into Coghill, Port Wales through Culross Passage, and on down to Chenega Island.

On this trip I saw results of the earthquake. This was my first time to see the damage that the tsunami had caused to my village. I saw that Ed Vlasoff's smokehouse had survived, so I cleaned it out and turned it into a steam bath. After boating and living off the land for weeks, a hot steam bath was just what I needed. Later, I went to see Henry Selanoff, my first cousin, Mark and Charlie Selanoff's brother, who was in his boat, to see if he wanted to come in and steam with me. But he was superstitious about the devastation of our village, and he refused to come to shore. Like others, he was frightened by the tragedy of the year before.

I recall a spring seal hunt with my father years later. We went to Port Wales with Frenchie Eleshansky and his family. It was on that seal hunt that I saw Frenchie wearing a necklace of dead hummingbirds as a good-luck charm. I remember another time when Frenchie made a boat with spruce pitch and pushed it into the Sound to help make the rain depart.

As a result of the tsunami, the National Disaster Agency came to the relief of the people once again, this time to give us a choice of rebuilding on Chenega or in the neighboring village of Tatitlek. They negotiated with the people of Chenega and came to the decision of rebuilding in Tatitlek. Shortly thereafter, the Agency built new two-bedroom homes with oil-burning stoves, lights, and refrigerators. These homes were better than any of the people had ever owned. Chenega had none of those modern conveniences. The only lights in the Sound were in the canneries of Nellie Juan, San Juan, and Crab Bay, which were operated by generators, turned by water of the nearby creeks.

So the people of Chenega Island chose to relocate and rebuild in Tatitlek. Two different groups with different ideas and different ways were now brought together and left to live. In the following years, I watched the survivors of Chenega slowly die of alcohol-related deaths. Many died in Cordova. Some of the people that died were my mentors who had taught me how to survive.

Mickey Eleshansky was found floating in the boat harbor in Cordova. Pete Kompkoff, Sr., was found floating in the boat harbor. Nick Eleshansky, Mickey's older brother, was found on his boat in the harbor—self-inflicted gunshot. Eddie Vlasoff also died in Cordova of a self-inflicted death. Dorothy "Tiny" Eleshansky died in Cordova. George Charanoff died in Cordova. My father, John Selanoff, was found dead in late springtime on a bench in Cordova.

These lonely deaths were the result of a People displaced from their homeland village, a People with no place to call home. I think it was partly because of the strength of belief in the superstitions that seems so alive to the people of Chenega. I think for many, the destruction of the old village was a sign of sorts, and so they kept away from their homeland.

Kenny Selanoff
And the Waters Shall Come

LIFE IN CHENEGA couldn't have been better. The people of Chenega were and still are a people of unity. Our elders are our strength. They unite us. It is they who keep our traditions alive. From one generation to the next, our traditions and our history survive.

I recall that March 27 was beautiful. It was calm and sunny. The day did not give any hint of the disaster to come. In fact, just before everything started there was an eerie calm, as if somebody had turned off all the world's sound. I was twelve years old. School was let out early that day, I think on account of Good Friday. That evening, we were going to watch *The House on Haunted Hill*. Every now and then we got to watch a movie.

My brothers—Paul (we call him Timmy), George and Billy—and I went down to play on the beach. Our sister, Jeanne, was with us. We were chasing little snowbirds. It was something to do. I remember that we went different directions along the beach. Billy and Jeanne went the other way. After a while, my brother Timmy was way out further than the rest of us. All of a sudden there was this rumbling, thunderous noise. It sounded like screaming jets flying fast and low overhead. It was deafening. Then the ground started shaking really hard. The ground dropped out from under my feet. I was really scared. I didn't know what was happening. I had never been in a big earthquake before. I didn't know what to think. I certainly didn't know anything about tsunamis.

George and I were standing right at the water's edge. The tide started receding really fast. I had never seen anything like it. Then, because the ground was shaking so much, the bay looked like it was boiling, just like a pot of boiling water.

I looked over toward our village, and I could see my dad, Charley Selanoff, frantically waving his arms at us. He was yelling something, but I couldn't hear what he was saying. I could see people standing outside John Totemoff's warehouse, which he had converted into a pool hall of sorts. I could also see Mikey Eleshansky running down to the dock to check on his skiff.

Finally, after what seemed like ages, the earth stopped shaking and the loud rumbling subsided a little, though there was still a roaring sound. In truth, the shaking lasted less than five minutes. I could just barely hear my father now. He was yelling at us to run up hill. I didn't know what to do. I didn't know about tidal waves. Instead, I ran out further on the point toward Timmy, yelling at him to run uphill. I don't know if he heard me.

I turned around and saw that my brother George was just standing on the beach as if he was in a frozen trance. He must have been really scared. I can still remember the sheer terror in his eyes. I started running around in circles. I must have been disoriented from the loud noise and the shaking ground. We were near what we called the White Rock over by the waterfall along the beach. The water in the bay was really bubbling and receding. It was really a strange thing to see.

I looked back, and my dad was still standing there yelling to us.

"Run!" he yelled. "Run and don't look back!"

I could see Mike Eleshansky running back up the dock. He was running fast, like a rabbit. I knew something must be really wrong for him to run like that and for my dad to be yelling so much. I turned and yelled to Timmy one last time. I screamed for him to run up hill, and then I started to run myself, hanging on to my brother George.

The water was still boiling and writhing. It was truly indescribable.

It was difficult to run on the beach. The ground was shaking and dropping from under me. It was made more difficult because I was trying to hold on to my brother.

When the first wave began to build in the distance, I could feel its fury as the hair on the back of my neck stood up. My father was still yelling and motioning for us to hurry up.

"Run faster!" he screamed.

There was a tall bulkhead at the village waterfront. It must have been a dozen feet tall. Maybe higher. There were stairs that led from the top down to the beach. I shoved my brother up the stairs. My father reached down and grabbed me. Without realizing it, I was flying through the air as he yanked me up. He told me to run uphill and not to look back. As we ran, we passed Moll-Look (I think she was Jack Evanoff's wife). I clearly remember her asking my father to help her. He turned back to help the old woman, but he told us to keep running ahead.

The first wave hit right after that. It sounded like a thunderclap when it struck the bulkhead wall.

We reached Daria Kompkoff's clothesline pole and held on to it. Because my dad was somewhere behind me, I thought surely he was gone. I could see my mother run into our house to get my baby sister, Mootie. Her real name is Evelyn, but we called her Mootie. I also saw my Aunt Dora with her daughter, Arvella, run back into her house, which was a little ways below our house. The first wave took her entire house. It was just taken out to sea. I never saw them again.

Then the second wave struck. It flooded over my brother and me as we clung to that clothesline pole. It was during that second wave that I saw most of the tragedies. As I hung on—wet and cold and frightened—I saw Daria, Willie Kompkoff, and my nephew, Philip Totemoff, trying to cross the small bridge that crossed the ravine and the tumbling stream that ran through our village. They were trying to get to their house. The force of the wave smashed them against their own house. It was terrible. I can still imagine it today as if it only just happened. The wave carried their entire house away, sweeping it and them out to sea.

At the same time, I could see Willie and Sally Evanoff and their granddaughter, Joanne Kompkoff trying to get out of their house. They were standing inside the doorway of the little arctic entry attached to front of their house. The wave pushed them back inside, and I never saw them again.

The Day That Cries Forever

The third wave hit when we were up near Steve Vlasoff's house behind the church. Mrs. Vlasoff would not leave her house, even though Margaret Borodkin, Richard Kompkoff, and my mother (Katie Selanoff) tried desperately to persuade her to leave. The last time I saw them, they were being swept away with the house. (I think it was a warehouse of sorts.) I remember Mrs. Vlasoff was still clutching her suitcase, and Richard Kompkoff was trying to reach both her and her daughter. In a blink of an eye he vanished. It was that fast and that terrible. The wave just grabbed him and pulled him under. He didn't have a chance.

My mother tried to go back down to help my dad, who was saving my sister, Nancy. I was now holding my little sister, Mootie, under my arms. She wanted to go with my parents, but I knew she would be a hindrance, so I held on to her. I knew that the swirling torrent of water and debris would hinder my father enough. He didn't need to worry about Mootie, too.

Later, I remember sitting safely on the hill with my mom, George, Mootie, Nancy, and Doreen Eleshansky. I don't remember how Doreen ended up with us, and I don't recall who brought Nancy up, either. It was probably my dad. We all sat up there watching the turmoil. Doreen told us to pray and keep praying. The water just kept rising, so we made our way up to the schoolhouse. But the water kept rising, so the elders told us to move even higher up the hill.

Little by little, one by one or in pairs, people started showing up. There were aftershocks all night. It seemed like they would never end. That night, around 9 P.M., I heard someone hollering. It was my brother, Timmy. I couldn't believe it. I didn't think he had made it, but there he was. Somehow, he had made it up the steep hill near the beach. You have to see how steep it is to believe it.

The thing I have never forgotten and will never forget was watching all that debris piled up in the bay floating away. The whole village was in it, every piece of lumber and furniture. People. Everything. It was all floating in the bay out front of where the village once stood.

And the Waters Shall Come

It's been forty years since that terrible day. I've been watching the tragedy in Indonesia on television, and I know from experience what they went through. I know that there was nothing they could do to save their loved ones. It's heart wrenching to watch helplessly.

〰〰

Paul Timothy Selanoff
The Day I Was Alone, but Not Alone

I REMEMBER ON THE DAY of the earthquake we were all going to watch a movie. It was *The House on Haunted Hill*. Before movie time, my dad and them just took a bath, and they were relaxing in the house. There was Mom and Willy. But I remember my oldest brother, Kenny, just wanted to go kill birds. So we went out on the beach, and we were chasing them. I was trying to get them first just so I could beat him, since he was older than me. I started getting way ahead on the beach. I was way out there all by myself, maybe a mile away from everybody. The village was real small from way out there. Even the other kids—there was Kenny, and Jerry and Georgie, I think—they were far away. I was all alone. I was way out there where the big boulders are. It was low tide.

All of a sudden the ground started shaking real hard. It was shaking so hard that those boulders were jumping off the ground like rubber balls. I started running back as fast as I could. I was wearing a black jacket with rocks in the pockets. As I ran, I jumped from boulder to boulder while they were bouncing in the air. I could hear Kenny and them yelling, "Come on! Come on!" But they were so far away I could barely hear them. Pretty soon I could hear this big rumble, a roaring like ten fighter jets flying by low. It was really loud. I got scared and started running faster. I was running and jumping from rock to rock, trying to get back to the village.

The ground was like Jell-O.

I was really scared, and then I felt a tap on my right shoulder, and I heard someone tell me not to be afraid. He tapped me and said,

The Day I Was Alone, but Not Alone

"Look, don't be afraid." Suddenly, all of my fears just went like still waters. Everything was calm and peaceful. There was no fear. Everything was calm. Everything was okay. And then He tapped me again and said the same thing. Then He tapped me a third time and said, "Look, don't be afraid."

I remember I turned around to look and there was a giant tidal wave, maybe a hundred feet tall, and it was almost upon me. So I turned around, but yet I wasn't scared. But I was still too far away and there was no place to go. There was a side of the mountain that was almost straight up. I couldn't run along the beach, so I had to go up the mountainside. I had to go straight up. I ran up as fast and as high as I could. There were no trees there. I think from an earlier snow slide. I had my right hand dug in. I recall the ground was really like Jell-O. When I ran up, I was holding on to a twig. It was just a thin little root or something sticking out of the ground. It broke, but I didn't fall. I don't know what it was. It was a powerful feeling, though, like someone holding me from falling.

I don't remember what happened after that. It's as if I fell asleep, as if somebody erased that time from my memory. I don't know how I escaped the wall of water. Since 1964, I've been thinking about it, trying to remember. I've come to think that He didn't want me to remember it, that there was no need to worry about it. Anyhow, that's how I've come to feel about that day. I just put it in His hands.

Later, I awoke on top of that mountain, saying "The Lord's Prayer." It was like He was setting a stage for me, like I was going to watch a movie all by myself. He had a little place for me to sit down. It was a depression on the ground like a natural armchair.

From it, I could just sit and see the waves coming towards the village. Down below, I could see someone running. I think it was Mike Eleshansky. He was running around on the dock checking on his skiff, and people were screaming at him. I saw Steve Eleshansky going around the point to John Selanoff's place. I watched Mrs. Evanoff and Joann Kompkoff run into a house and close the door. And then the first wave came and went, and I saw three people riding in and out on the waves on this log. I think it was the light pole from the church. I come to find out later it was my dad and Kenny and somebody else. They rode out all three waves.

In between the second and the third wave, the water went out so far that the whole bay just emptied out and became mudflats. I looked below at the village again and said, "What the heck?" There was this one guy running down, and there was someone stuck in the mud way down there. I didn't know who it was. You can't imagine how far down it was. But he ran down there and pulled the person out.

It turned out it was my dad and the person he saved was my sister, Nancy.

Then, the next wave came in, and it washed right up the hill where the village was. It swept all around it. It was way up there. The whole village was under water. It was two feet deep in the light plant (generator) up on the hill. A funny thing about it: there was my dad's boat—maybe eighteen feet long. It was named Jeanie. It was running around like it was full speed going fifty or sixty miles an hour as if someone was inside steering it. It was racing around all over. When it was all over—after the three waves had come and gone—it was parked right where it was supposed to be, without an anchor, not even broke, like nothing had happened at all. It must have got a hole, though, because it slowly sank there. Its bones are still down there.

From atop the hill, I saw the St. Theresa get hit by two waves coming together. It was Eddie Vlasoff's boat. At first it was sitting on the mudflat because all the water went out of the bay before the big waves hit. When the wave came in, it lifted that boat right up and pushed it up in the air above the trees, annihilating it right before my eyes.

After the third and last wave, I remember the whole bay was full of debris, logs and lumber and parts of houses and boats and everything just going out to sea. Next thing I remember was hearing someone yelling for help. I stood up so I could see better and there was Margaret Borodkin floating out there among all that debris. I was too far away to hear what she was yelling, but I knew it was her. I recognized her voice. It looked like she was stuck in the debris, like it was crushing her. In a little while, I saw a boat trying to get to her, pushing its way through all the debris. Eventually, George Borodkin, I think, came in his skiff and got her.

The old church was destroyed. But later they found the Bible from the church near the wreckage, and it was lying there open to a passage from Revelation. We still have that Bible in the new Russian Orthodox Church in Chenega Bay.

I still remember how powerful those waves were. You can't imagine what it's like to see three giant waves, each almost a hundred feet tall, maybe higher, coming in at hundreds of miles per hour, maybe faster—a giant wall just coming in like that, that fast. It's just awesome. No words can describe it. I hope you never experience a thing like that.

I sat up on the hill for maybe two more hours. It was getting dark, and I could see only two lights left on in the village—Ms. Madsen's and Norma Selanoff's, who were maybe alive up at the schoolhouse. There were no other lights at all. I thought they were the only other two people left on earth. I really thought it was the end of the world. But I wasn't afraid. I remember that I was still calm, sitting up there on the hill in the snow.

I finally made my way along the hill around our village to look for people up near the school, walking in snow up to my waist. I was cold, I had lost a shoe, and I was tired. I got scared and started calling through the darkness. Someone answered. I ran downhill towards the voice, jumping over debris. I must have jumped eight feet at a time. I followed that voice, and guess who it was? It was my dad. When I saw him I jumped, almost flying, into his arms like a magnet.

He hugged me and whispered in my ear, "You seen Buttons and Gula?" He almost cried. But he was happy to see me. I was so happy to see my dad.

Later, everyone who was left was up in the woods up above the schoolhouse huddled around a campfire. That night I slept in one of those old Blazo fuel boxes—one of those wooden crates—listening to my mom crying. There weren't many blankets or extra coats. All we had was whatever we were already wearing or what was in the school at the time. We used whatever we could find to keep warm.

The Day That Cries Forever

The next day, we started walking down the hill to where the village had been. We were at the schoolhouse when another big earthquake shook, almost knocking everyone down, and we all went running back up the hill again. We thought another wave was coming. We were like scared little rabbits. I could tell even the men were scared, which was really different. They were never scared of anything.

It was perhaps ten minutes after the first earthquake hit that the waves began to come in. It might have been longer. I don't remember for certain. Everything happened so fast. So many things happened to so many people in just a few minutes. There was no time.

We lost lots of people that day.

I remember when the planes came to take us away after the second day. When we were up in the air, I looked down at my village and there was nothing left except the old schoolhouse on the top of the hill. There was nothing left. I remember as we flew over Knight Island, I looked out the window and saw all these orange things floating on the surface. I thought they were crab buoys. I remember thinking, "Man, they're crabbing all over." But it was red snappers that had died in the tidal waves and were floating around everywhere.

No one lived in Chenega after that. Everyone moved away to other places.

A few years after the earthquake, my family went back to visit the village for the first time. We were fishing aboard Nellie Juan 36, and we stopped to see our old home. I remember it was dark outside when we dropped anchor just off the beach. Then the strangest thing happened. It was strange, but it was also comforting at the same time. It was more mystery than anything else. There was this dishpan hanging on the wall near the door about four feet from me—maybe six feet. All of a sudden, the pan started making sound like someone was banging on it. The thing was bouncing and swinging against the wall, but the sea was calm and flat. The boat wasn't rocking at all. I thought it was a trick, but no one else was there. Mom and dad were on the beach walking around with Tommy. I told George to look, and he also saw it just bouncing around, making sound like someone was banging it, like someone was using it like a drum. But I wasn't afraid. I had the sense that every one of the twenty-three souls of those lost relatives was happy to see us come home. They were drumming to welcome us home. They were happy to see us.

I guess I was a little scared.

Other strange things happened, too. We could hear what sounded like people walking around up on the deck. Things were being moved around like a washbasin that we found out on the deck by the winch. And then someone or something untied our anchor line, and you could hear it running out. My dad said, "That's enough," as he caught the line just before it went over the side. We slept there the next night too, but nothing happened. It was quiet. They had come to visit us that one time, all at once, really hard. You could hear them all over that first night, but it was quiet from then on.

I guess they got to say goodbye.

≈

Jessie Tiedeman
A Twist of Fate

I was in Cordova when the earthquake hit. I was thirty-eight years old, and I remember our boat was leaking so we were in the harbor trying to repair the leak. My husband and our two sons were trying to fix the boat. Even though my family lived in Tatitlek, we had just been to Chenega two days before.

When the earthquake hit, I remember everything was shaking, the tide went out far, and the exposed mudflat was like jelly. It was really a strange thing to watch. The tide went in and out several times, like a river. The shaking lasted for a long time. We couldn't even stand up. Everyone was just trying to hold on. I remember I was so scared. Everyone was scared. After the earthquake, it was fairly quiet. I don't even recall hearing dogs barking or people yelling or anything. Even though the ground had shook really hard, I didn't see any nearby buildings collapse.

Pretty soon someone came by and told us that we had to get up to higher ground. He said there was a tidal wave warning. So we went up the hill and met up with people we knew. From up there, we could see how far the tide had gone out. It was amazing. Then, in no time at all, the tide came back in and I could see our boat was drifting away. It had come loose from the grid and was adrift out in the bay. But some fellow was kind enough to save our boat for us.

There never was much of a tidal wave in Cordova. I guess the island must have protected the town.

Later, after we thought it was safe, we all went back down the hill. The town looked okay. The only building that was lost was the clam diggers building, which was washed out to sea at Whiteshed.

A Twist of Fate

I learned later that the earthquake had done little to Tatitlek. I heard that the Narrows had dried up a couple of times when the tide went out, leaving the boats high and dry, but that the water came back in and the boats were okay. It didn't destroy any of the buildings or anything. I also learned that my uncle, Alex Chimovisky, his son, Immanuel, and his daughter, Anna, had died at Nellie Juan. The tidal wave must have hit real hard there. They never did find them.

The earthquake changed our land. Afterwards, there were fewer clams, crabs, and cockles. It really affected the razor clam beds down around Cordova and the Copper River flats. It hit our seals, too. Seal hunters had to go far away to find seal meat after the earthquake. It took most of our subsistence foods.

It was so sad.

I felt really bad for all the people of Chenega. They lost so much that day, so many people. They lost everything. I guess we were just fortunate to have been in Cordova at the time.

Maggie A. Totemoff
What Will Remain

I WAS BORN IN CHENEGA in May of 1923, which means that I was almost forty-one years old on Good Friday of 1964. We had a very big family. I had five brothers: Eddie, John, George, Paul, and Spiridon; and three sisters: Margaret, Sally, and Flora. I attended school in the village. When I was older I helped the teachers in the small schoolhouse.

My mother was a homemaker, and my father was a lay reader in the church. Occasionally, he worked at LaTouche. Many of us worked seasonally for the salmon cannery at Nellie Juan and Port Ashton. It seems like summers were always the same: everyone went to their fish camps at Port Wells or Shipyard. We'd catch salmon to put up for the long winter. Some of the men would shoot seals for their snouts. They would go to Icy Bay in bidarkas or motorized skiffs. Some of the younger men, even boys, would go with them. They got paid a certain price for each seal they shot. I don't remember how much, but it seemed like a lot of money back then.

There used to be quite a few boats moored in the bay out front of the village. I believe the villagers had half a dozen Nellie Juan ("NJ") boats in the harbor.

My mother went to Valdez one summer, and she brought back a piece of birch tree. I think it was a birch tree. We didn't have any trees like that in Chenega. She planted it. She was very protective of that little sapling. Even today, you can see that tree. It's the largest and most obvious thing you'll see when you go to the old village. During a memorial trip to the old Chenega village site, I took a piece of that tree and planted it in the new village at Chenega Bay. Nowadays, it's taller than our house!

The Russian Orthodox Church was, and still is, a major part of our life. In the spring, men used to go collect loads of clean gravel, which they spread around the church grounds to make it look nice. The ladies would decorate the inside of the church. I remember both Larry Evanoff's mother and Fred Kompkoff's mother would make lots of crepe-paper flowers, which they placed all around the church and its gilded icons. It was so beautiful!

On Good Friday, all of the dogs in the village would be rounded up and taken in a skiff out to an island in the bay out front of the village. I think it was to keep them out of the way of religious celebrations.

During Russian Christmas, the men and women would walk around the village carrying a large star, singing songs. I remember we had our own stars—one just for women and one just for men. A lot of things were divided up like that back then. Sometimes we'd meet each other and sing songs in the cold.

Once a year or so, a bishop would come from Juneau or Sitka to hold services in Chenega. Maybe twice a year a traveling priest would come and hold services.

Michael John Vigil
The Unforgotten

I WAS ALMOST BORN on Nellie Juan 37 in 1953. That's one of the fishing boats we operated for the Nellie Juan cannery. The boat was just coming around Sawmill Point when my uncle, fearing that my mother was about to give birth to me, yelled, "Hold on, Arlene! I see lights ahead." Luckily, she was able to hold off, and I was born on land in what is now the Prince William Motel in Cordova.

I lived in Chenega until I was almost ten years old. It was a great place to grow up. I remember we used to really live off the land. We picked all kinds of berries. We gathered wild bird eggs, clams, and shellfish. The men used to hunt and fish. The whole village came together to gather enough food for everyone. We used just about everything on the land or in the sea in one way or another.

Life was good and simple and happy, and resources were abundant.

In such a close-knit community, everyone cared for each other. Everyone cared and everyone shared. It was an overriding rule. It wasn't so much a rule; it was simply the way of things.

I remember the day the airplane—I think it was a Widgeon—came in to fly me out of the old village. Umma (my grandmother) made me put on my best Sunday clothes. The plane was only for me. No one else was leaving. I knew something was wrong, so I ran away and hid until the airplane left. The next day, another charter plane arrived. My uncle John had to pick me up and carry me because I didn't want to go. Eventually, I was flown all the way to Denver, Colorado, where my parents had moved. We stayed there for less than a year. Then my father transferred to Seattle to work for Hertz, the car rental company.

The Unforgotten

16. Fish from the sea (Sam Ribaloff)

On the first school day after the Alaska Earthquake—I must have been eleven—I remember my counselor came into the classroom and spoke to my teacher. They kept looking at me as they spoke, but I

The Day That Cries Forever

didn't know what they were talking about. I thought I was in trouble. It wouldn't have been a surprise. I felt like I didn't belong in the Western world. I belonged in my village. Then the teacher told me to go to the main office with the counselor. There, in private, he told me the news about Chenega; how a series of tidal waves had destroyed the village and claimed many lives.

School personnel gave my siblings and me a ride home. When I walked in the front door, my mother was sitting on the floor crying. There was nothing we could do. We were too far away from our families, and there was no way to contact any of them. All we could do was wait and pray.

My dad came home from work early, which was something he never did. The whole family sat by the phone for the rest of the day and night waiting for the phone to ring with news, good or bad. But it never did.

I'll never forget that day.

Even though the old village has been gone now for over forty years, I count myself fortunate and blessed to have grown up there. I will always remember Chenega and the people of Chenega with fondness.

They will never be forgotten.

Donia M. Abbott
Touched My Generation

EACH YEAR ON Memorial Day, my people travel back to Chenega to visit the place where our roots were pulled. We go there to honor those who perished in the 1964 earthquake. The annual journey is spiritual, uplifting, sad, hurtful, joyous, and informing. It is a homecoming where memories are happy, sad, and plentiful. They mourn the loss of their loved ones, reminisce with one another, sharing stories of growing up, and they remember what life used to be like in the old days before the ocean showed its wrath.

In 1964 the people of Chenega, my people, suffered great loss. On a quiet afternoon in Prince William Sound, a community of less than one hundred people lost twenty-six of their own. Mothers, fathers, brothers, sisters, aunts, uncles, sons, and daughters were lost to the sea. The three waves wiped out everything, except the school building, which stands even today as testimony that there was once beautiful life on an island that holds many dark secrets, secrets made by the three waves that stripped the village of everything: its people, their trust, their feelings, and most importantly their home. My people were forced to move away from the only home they had ever known. They were forced out of their comfort zones, forced to live in different communities, places they once visited but never imagined they would one day call home. My people were homeless for twenty years, dispersed throughout Alaska and as far away as Washington.

The devastation that hit Chenega in 1964 impacted every family, including mine.

The Day That Cries Forever

17. Chenega Village schoolhouse, 1997

My mother was three years old when the waves came. As you can imagine, I was not born yet, but the pain and suffering caused by the earthquake has affected my generation as well. My grandparents, The Very Reverend Nicholas and Matushka Mary Kompkoff, lost two of their daughters in the tsunami. Norma Jean and Julia Ann would have been my aunts. Their deaths left my siblings and me with no aunts on our mother's side of the family. It has always been painful knowing that both of my aunts were swept away in one of the three waves that hit Chenega.

I have often wondered what my life would be like if they had survived. I have watched my Gramma mourn the loss of her daughters ever since I was about ten years old. I have heard her tell many stories about the two of them. She cries often, wondering what their life might have been and how many grandchildren they might have given her. I have witnessed firsthand the pain and suffering of my family for the loss of their daughters and sisters. I could never imagine losing my child or my sister. I believe the tears shed for them are tears of such a deep sadness that the sorrow can never be fully explained, only recognized.

I remember as a little girl being very excited to go to Chenega. Over the years, my excitement turned to sadness as I realized what my people had suffered. I remember combing the beaches for treasures, seeing the "huge" waterfall, and seeing the "Tarzan Tree." To me, the broken pieces of glass, marbles, broken dishes, and other things I found were treasures. I remember showing them to my Gramma. One was an old piece of a dish that had floral designs on it. She recognized the dishes and remembered whom they belonged to, which amazed me. I now realize that the treasures I found were once the possessions of people who lost everything. It is sad to think that the things I found on the beach may have been all that remained of a shattered life. I still search the beaches for treasures in hopes that my Gramma can identify something that belonged to her or someone else in my family.

As a little girl, I thought the waterfall at the end of the beach was the hugest waterfall I had ever seen. We always played in it because it would be so hot when we went to Chenega. I remember hearing stories about the "Tarzan Tree" from middle-aged adults today who said as children they spent much of their time playing on this huge tree that had a rope, which they would use to swing like Tarzan. I would always be exited to see it, knowing that is where my aunts, uncles, and other family members spent countless hours of their youth playing.

Returning to Chenega always leaves an unexplainable feeling in the pit of my stomach. I have always wished that it could have been the place I called home. Growing up in Chenega Bay was wonderful, but I cannot help having the feeling that if the earthquake had not wiped out the original village of Chenega, life would have been drastically different. I feel this way because I have listened to stories my Gramma has told me for the past twenty years. She always claimed that if the "old ones" were still around things would be different. She says there would still be the sense of community within our people and that we would not be divided, as we are today. She tells me over and over about the importance of caring for our elders as they did in the old days. She says that the church was the center of the community and especially during holidays and that the "men folk" in the village would make sure that the church was glowing and beautiful. On Sunday mornings, everyone attended the church service. Today, in Chenega Bay there are about sixty people and on Sunday mornings, there are less than ten people in attendance.

My Gramma always says that people in Chenega used to help each other with everything. She said that when men went out for fish or seal, everyone in the village got a piece of the catch. In Chenega Bay today, few people go out to hunt or fish. The subsistence way of life that used to be so important is slowly being lost to today's McDonalds, Burger King, Taco Bell, and other modern and easily accessible foods.

Many of the people who were lost in the earthquake would be elders today, guiding us in a more positive direction. I believe that life in Chenega would have carried on the way it always had been if we were still in Chenega and not transplanted to Chenega Bay. After listening to the stories my Gramma has told me about the strong unity our people once had, it has left me with an uneasy feeling that the 1964 earthquake affected not only those who lived through it, but also the generations to come. It created a void that will never be filled.

Twenty years after my people were forced by nature to leave their home in Chenega, they were again faced with disaster, this time man-made. I was eight years old in 1989, when the Exxon Valdez wrecked, spilling millions of gallons of crude oil into Prince William Sound. I recall there was a rush of people who came through Chenega Bay—reporters, laborers, executives, famous people, and just those who were curious about my village. I remember there was a boat docked in our harbor after the spill, filled with food, as if that food was supposed to replace the salmon, seal, sea lion, and shellfish that the sea had provided for us. We were told not to eat anything from the sea for the next ten years. Many people did not wait that long because they could not live without our traditional foods. The oil still remains just below the surface of the beaches, but there is nothing we can do. We Chenega people have been faced with two terrible disasters in the past forty-one years. But, I believe they have made us a stronger people; we just need to learn how to embrace our power in order to overcome these obstacles.

We need the trip home to Chenega each year to recognize that although we have been faced with horrendous challenges, challenges from up above, we need to unite in order to cope with the losses we have suffered. We need the trip home to help begin the healing process. Many of those who lived through the earthquake still have difficulties talking about their feelings. I believe that as difficult as it may be to discuss the events of March 27, 1964, my people must get it off their chest in order to move on. I also know that many of us who lived through the 1989 Exxon Valdez Oil Spill are angry for many reasons. We have a right to be angry. The environmental disaster, the largest in American history, could have been prevented.

Chenega people are strong. We were born and raised to be strong. We are survivors. We have much to be proud of. We need to recognize that we are one people. We need to make our ancestors smile upon us by uniting as one community. The obstacles in our daily lives weaken our powers. We are weighed down by drug and alcohol abuse, corrosive politics, stubbornness, and, most importantly, a lack of forgiveness. We need to re-learn forgiveness. We need to listen to the elders we have left, instead of living our lives without their guidance. We need to recognize that we were never a drunken or stoned people. We lived off the land, taking pride in our heritage and land. We lived harmoniously with one another, helping one another. We were a community. We need to return to our roots and closely examine them, learn who we really are, because what is happening today would never have happened had we been living life as our ancestors did in Chenega. For the well-being of future generations, we need to show our strength and not let the obstacles with which we have been faced do any more damage than they already have.

Notes on the Contributors

Margaret Borodkin is proud of her four granddaughters and eight great grandchildren.

Steve Eleshansky lives in Eagle River with his wife, Ella. They have two children and five grandchildren.

Bill Hjort lives in Edmonds, Washington.

Karen Selanoff Katelnikoff was born in Tatitlek but raised in Chenega. Her mother was originally from Tatitlek. She was attending school in Wrangell when the Good Friday Earthquake struck. For the past two decades, she has worked to preserve the Aleut language. She currently lives in Tatitlek with her husband, Phillip, and their dog, Batman. She still teaches language and dance in the school.

Carol Ann Kompkoff is a full blood Sugpiat Alutiiq from the Chaniiqmiut Tribe. She has lived most of her life in Prince William Sound. Her parents and grandparents taught her to cherish and respect the land, the environment, and, most importantly, its people. The youngest of six siblings, she has four children and currently resides in Chenega Bay with her husband, Charles Robertson. She is proud of her fifteen years of sobriety.

Donald Kompkoff, Sr., was born in 1938 on Chenega Island. He attended Mt. Edgecumbe Boarding School for Alaska Natives in Sitka for two years, before moving to Valdez, where he graduated from Valdez

High School in 1960. He later moved to Tatitlek where he married Gail Totemoff in 1966. He has spent his life hunting and fishing in the area around Chenega.

Joyce Kompkoff was raised in Chenega Bay, Cordova, Tatitlek, and Anchorage, where she graduated from high school. She became interested in health care and emergency medical services. She lives in Valdez, where she is an Oil Spill Response Technician. She has four beautiful children.

Mary Ann Kompkoff was born and raised on Chenega Island, moving only after the 1964 Earthquake caused her relocation to Cordova. She lived in Anchorage for twenty years. A widow for eighteen years, she lives in Chenega Bay. She has sixteen grandchildren and seventeen great-grandchildren.

Paul Kompkoff, Jr., has been a commercial fisherman for over forty-five years. He still subsistence hunts and fishes for his family. He also serves on the Chenega Corporation Board of Directors. He has lived in Anchorage for the past twelve years but also maintains a home in Chenega Bay.

Pete Kompkoff, Jr., was born and raised at Kake Cove on Chenega Island. He lived there until 1957. He attended the Mt. Edgecumbe boarding school for almost two years, then moving to Valdez and graduating from Valdez High School in 1961. That fall he joined the Navy and was honorably discharged in 1965. He moved to Tacoma, Washington, where he earned a certificate in highway civil engineering. Later, he attended Shasta College and earned an associate's degree. He has served on many important state committees and boards. Presently, he is a tribal administrator for the Chenega IRA Council.

Henry Makarka was born in Cordova in 1930. He has fished commercially for most of his life and worked in construction and as a laborer.

Notes on Contributors

He served in the Army from 1952 to 1954 during the Korean War. He has been married for thirty-four years.

Andy Selanoff was born in Chenega around 1926. He lived there until 1956 to work as a deckhand. Later, he moved to Sitka to work at Mt. Edgecumbe School. From there he moved to Edmonton, Alberta, and then back to Alaska where he has resided ever since.

Paul T. Selanoff, "Timmy" to his family, "Tim-moo-ska" to elders, is the son of Charles W. Selanoff. He has many children. He has fished and hunted around Chenega all his life. After all these decades, he is still homesick.

John E. Smelcer is a shareholder of Ahtna Native Corporation and Tazlina Village Traditional Council. He was the Executive Director of the Ahtna Heritage Foundation, where he worked with elders to produce a series of oral history collections and language curriculum materials, including *The Ahtna Noun Dictionary* and *In the Shadows of Mountains*, a collection of traditional stories. He is the only tribal member able to read, write, and speak Ahtna. Over the past fifteen years, he has taught at universities around the world and studied advanced English literature at Cambridge University. He is the author of twenty-six books.

Charles W. Totemoff was nine months old when the tsunamis hit Chenega during the 1964 Alaska Earthquake. He has lived in Tatitlek, Cordova, Chenega Bay, and Anchorage. He has earned two master's degrees, including a MBA from Alaska Pacific University, where he was recently appointed a trustee. Since 1988 he has served as chairman and CEO of Chenega Corporation. He has a wonderful daughter, Amber.

Maggie Totemoff lives in Chenega Bay. She enjoys picking berries and watching spawning salmon fill the creeks in the village.

Michael J. Vigil was born in Cordova in 1953 to a mother of Aleut and

Russian descent and a father of Spanish and French heritage. He was raised in Chenega until he was ten. His family then moved to Colorado so that he wouldn't have to attend an Indian boarding school. He later dropped out of college to become a carpenter's apprentice. After fourteen years as a carpenter, he moved to Chenega Bay to become a tribal administrator and tribal council member.

Donia Wilson-Abbott was born in Anchorage in 1981. Her parents are Carol Ann Kompkoff and Philip Hunter Wilson, Sr. She was raised in Chenega Bay where she lived with her grandparents, Father Nicholas and Matushka Mary Kompkoff, who taught her the importance of the church and respect for the elders. She deeply values her native culture.